INSTANT POT AIR FRYER LID COOKBOOK 2020

EASY AND DELICIOUS INSTANT POT AIR FRYER LID RECIPES FOR FAST AND HEALTHY MEALS. (ROAST, BAKE, BROIL AND DEHYDRATE)

CONTENTS

INTRODUCTION

The Air Fryer Lid brings a whole new set of skills to your kitchen, making it fun and easy for anyone to prepare great healthy meals — fast. Whip up tender ribs or a nice big chicken in your Instant Pot, then use the Air Fryer Lid to give every morsel a beautiful finish. Air Fry, Broil, Bake, Roast, Reheat and Dehydrate directly in the Instant Pot's inner pot for big savings on time, space and clean-up.

Conveniently, the Air Fryer Lid remains unattached to the cooker base, so it is easy to maneuver, easy to clean and comes with a protective pad for safe and easy storage. The lid's control panel features buttons for your various needs, and the display is bright and easy to read. 6 preset Smart Programs help you get cooking with just the touch of a button, or you can modify the settings for a totally customized cooking experience. After loads of rigorous testing the results are in... and they are delicious.

WHY INSTANT POT AIR FRYER LID

Bring on the heat
The Instant Pot Air Fryer Lid instantly transforms everyone's favorite pressure cooker into a 6-in-1 air fryer with a simple switch of the lid. One amazing machine, two innovative lids, infinite possibilities for taste and texture.

Cook and crisp
Swap out the pressure cooker lid for the innovative air fryer lid, and you've got a whole new set of cooking techniques available — all fast, easy, and available with the touch of a button.

One appliance, two lids, infinite possibilities
Simply swap out the regular pressure cooker lid for the innovative air fryer lid, and you've got a whole new set of cooking techniques available — all fast, easy, and available with the touch of a button.

Quick and healthy
Like pressure cooking, air frying helps you save time and cook healthy meals with amazing results — without using a lot of energy or heating up your kitchen. It's as easy as cook, lift, switch!

EvenCrisp technology
Get deep-fried taste and texture with little to no oil. EvenCrisp technology ensures tender juicy meals with a crisp, golden finish, every time. Now you can make perfect chicken wings, crispy French fries and onion rings, and golden battered vegetables the healthy way, using less than 2 tablespoons of oil.

Versatile and convenient
The Smart Programs make it fun and easy for anyone — whether it's your profession or you've never cooked a day in your life — to prepare great healthy meals fast. Choose a preset Smart Program, or customize the time and temperature for total control over your cooking, and save your presets so your favorite meals can be made the way you like them every time

Easy control, easy clean-up
With a big bright dual display and easy-to-use controls, selecting programs and making adjustments is a breeze — even during cooking. Clean-up is easy too. The

Air Fryer Lid's sleek surfaces wipe clean with a damp cloth, and the accessories are all dishwasher safe

FAQ: INSTANT POT AIR FRYER LID & FOOD

HOW DOES THE AIR FRYER LID WORK?

The Air Fryer Lid is the Instant Pot's best bud. It uses super-heated, fast-blowing air to cook and crisp food. You can use it to cook food from fresh or frozen, or, to crisp up an item after it's been cooked in the Instant Pot.

WHAT FOODS WORK BEST WITH THE AIR FRYER LID?

You can make all kinds of things with the Air Fryer Lid!
- Your favorite fried and pan-fried dishes, like sausage, schnitzel and steak
- Yummy baked dishes like pies and cakes
- Fresh or frozen convenience foods like fries, wings and mozza sticks are a snap
- Give a crispy, golden skin to pressure cooked chicken, or caramelize ribs to give them a nice crust
- Dehydrate fruits, vegetables and meat for fun fruit leather rollups and DIY jerky

Compared to a full-sized oven, the Air Fryer Lid is also a fast, convenient and energy-efficient way to reheat and re-crisp leftovers.

ARE THERE FOODS THAT CANNOT BE COOKED WITH THE AIR FRYER LID?

Almost anything you can cook in a conventional oven can be cooked with the Air Fryer Lid, but for best results always space out foods so air has room to circulate freely, and cook in small batches.

Avoid foods dipped in batter, such as calamari, tempura shrimp and buttermilk fried chicken. If you want breading, go for an egg wash and breadcrumb coating.

HOW MUCH FOOD CAN I COOK AT ONE TIME?

You can fit a lot in the inner pot, but for best results, remember to give your food room to breathe and don't crowd food items.

Place food items in a single layer or use the multi-level air fryer basket, and ensure there is room for the hot air to circulate freely.

DO I NEED TO PRE-HEAT THE AIR FRYER LID?

We recommend pre-heating the Air Fryer Lid and inner pot before adding most foods to the inner pot for cooking.

The only caveat is when using the Bake Smart Program. Due to the small cooking area, we recommend placing your baking dish in the inner pot before turning the Air Fryer Lid on.

WHAT HAPPENS IF I DON'T TURN MY FOOD WHEN REMINDED TO?

Depending on the Smart Program, the Air Fryer Lid may beep part way through to remind you to turn your food. If you don't lift the lid, the air fryer continues cooking at the selected temperature until the timer completes.

Depending on the food item, failing to turn your food may result in uneven cooking. Refer to the Troubleshooting table in the User Manual for further assistance.

IS THE AIR FRYER LID COMPATIBLE WITH ALL INSTANT POTS?

Use the Air Fryer Lid with the following 6 Quart Instant Pots:

Duo 60 (IP-DUO60, IP-DUO60 V2, IP-DUO60 V2.1, IP-DUO60-ENW, IP-DUO60 V3, Duo 60 V3, Duo Frontier Rose 60, Duo Dazzling Dahlia 60, Duo White 60, Duo Teal 60, Duo Red 60, Duo Black SS 60, Duo Red SS 60, Duo Nova Black SS 60). Duo Plus 60 (Duo Plus 60, Duo Plus Cinnamon SS 60, Duo Plus Blue SS 60, Duo Plus Copper SS 60, Duo Plus Black SS 60). Ultra 60 (Ultra 60). Viva 60 (Viva, Viva 60, Viva Cinnamon 60, Viva Cobalt 60, Viva Eggplant 60, Viva Red SS 60, Viva Black SS 60). Nova Plus 60 (Nova Plus 60). Duo Nova 60 (Duo Nova 60).

Air Fryer Lid is NOT compatible with the following models: Smart WiFi 60, Duo Evo Plus 6, Duo Evo Plus 60, Duo SV 60 or Max 60.

MY FOOD IS NOT CRISPY-WHAT AM I DOING WRONG?

Your Air Fryer Lid is designed to produce crispy, golden results without needing to submerge your food in oil, but for best results follow these guidelines:

- Pat dry moist food items (like potato or zucchini sticks) with a clean dish towel or paper towel
- Toss your food in up to 2 tablespoons of oil
- Preheat the air fryer to blast your food with hot air
- Turn or toss your food when reminded
- Use an egg wash and breadcrumb batter instead of loose liquid batters

Always follow a trusted recipe when air frying.

BREAKFAST RECIPES

BLUEBERRY MUFFINS

🕐 Cooking Time: 24 minutes   🧢 Serves: 8 Muffins

Ingredients:
- ⅔ cup blueberries, fresh or frozen and thawed
- 1⅓ cups flour
- 2 teaspoons baking powder
- ½ cup sugar
- ¼ teaspoon salt
- 1 egg
- ½ cup milk
- ⅓ cup canola oil
- 8 foil muffin cups including paper liners

Directions:
1. Combine the flour, baking powder, sugar, and salt in a bowl. Set aside.
2. Whisk together the egg, milk, and canola oil. Pour the egg mixture into the flour mixture. Stir to mix well, then fold in the blueberries.
3. Divide the mixture among 8 muffin cups. Arrange the muffins into the air fryer basket. You may need to work in batches to avoid overcrowding.
4. Put the air fryer lid on and cook in the preheated instant pot at 325°F for 14 minutes or until a toothpick inserted in the center comes out clean.
5. Remove the muffins from the basket and serve warm.

MUSHROOM AND EGG STUFFED PISTOLETTE ROLLS

⊕Cooking Time: 20 minutes   ⬤Serves: 4

Ingredients:
- ¼ cup fresh mushrooms, diced
- 4 eggs
- 4 pistolette rolls
- 1 teaspoon butter
- ½ teaspoon dried onion flakes
- ¼ teaspoon dried dill weed
- 1 tablespoon milk
- ¼ teaspoon dried parsley
- ½ teaspoon salt

Directions:
1. Coat a 6×6×2-inch baking pan with the butter. Add the mushrooms and onion. Place the pan in the air fryer basket.
2. Put the air fryer lid on and cook in the preheated instant pot at 400°F for 4 minutes. Shake the basket once when the lid screen indicates 'TURN FOOD' halfway through.
3. Whisk the eggs, dill, milk, parsley, and salt in a mixing bowl. Add the mixture into the pan and cook for 4 minutes more. Stir the mixture every 1 minute.
4. Meanwhile, cut a hole in the center of a pistolette roll, then Hollow it out and leave a ½-inch shell. Repeat with the remaining rolls.
5. Remove the pan from the basket. Use a spoon to stuff the rolls with the mixture.
6. Place the rolls in the basket. Put the lid on and cook at 400°F for 2 minutes until golden brown.
7. Remove from the basket and serve warm.

CORNMEAL AND HAM MUFFINS

⊕ Cooking Time: 10 minutes   Serves: 8 Muffins

Ingredients:
- ½ cup Cheddar cheese, shredded
- ¾ cup yellow cornmeal
- ½ cup ham, diced
- ¼ cup flour
- 1½ teaspoons baking powder
- ¼ teaspoon salt
- 1 egg, beaten
- ½ cup milk
- 2 tablespoons canola oil
- 8 foil muffin cups, liners removed and sprayed with cooking spray

Directions:
1. Combine the flour, baking powder, cornmeal, and salt in a bowl. Pour over the beaten egg, milk, and canola oil. Stir to mix well, then fold in the ham and cheese.
2. Spoon the mixture into 8 muffin cups. Arrange the cups in the air fryer basket. You may need to work in batches to avoid overcrowding.
3. Put the air fryer lid on and bake in the preheated instant pot at 400°F for 5 minutes, then lower the temperature and bake at 325°F for 1 minutes or until tops spring back when touched lightly.
4. Remove the muffins from the basket and serve warm.

SCRAMBLED EGG AND HAM MUFFINS

Cooking Time: 24 minutes   Serves: 4 Muffins

Ingredients:
- 1 cup Colby or Jack cheese, shredded
- 4 eggs
- 4 slices ham, diced
- Salt and freshly ground black pepper, to taste
- 4 English muffins, split in half crosswise
- Cooking spray

Directions:
1. Whisk the eggs, salt, and pepper in a bowl. Pour the whisked eggs into a greased 6×6×2-inch baking pan. Place the pan in the air fryer basket.
2. Put the air fryer lid on and cook in the preheated instant pot at 400°F for 5 minutes or until scrambled. Stir constantly during the cooking. Remove the pan from the basket. Allow to cool for a few minutes.
3. Spritz the air fryer basket with cooking spray. Arrange the bottom halves of the English muffins in the basket. Scatter half cup of the cheese on the muffins, then put a slice of ham on them. Spoon a quarter of scrambled eggs over each muffin, then top the eggs with remaining cheese.
4. Put the lid on and cook at 350°F for 1 minutes. Put the top halves of the muffins on them, flip the muffins and continue cooking for 4 minutes until the muffins are toasted.
5. Remove the muffins from the basket and serve warm.

FRENCH STYLE TOAST STICKS

Cooking Time: 12 minutes   Serves: 4

Ingredients:
- 2 eggs
- ½ cup milk
- ⅛ teaspoon salt
- ½ teaspoon pure vanilla extract
- ¾ cup cornflakes, crushed
- 1 tablespoon olive oil
- 6 slices white bread, each slice cut into 4 strips
- Cooking spray
- Honey, for dipping

Directions:
1. Whisk together the eggs, vanilla, milk, and salt in a bowl. Combine the cornflakes with olive oil in a separate bowl.
2. Dredge the bread strips into the egg mixture, then in the cornflakes. Shake the excess off.
3. Spritz the air fryer basket with cooking spray. Place the bread strips in the air fryer basket, and spritz them with cooking spray.
4. Put the air fryer lid on and cook in batches in the preheated instant pot at 400°F for 6 minutes or until well browned. Flip the bread strips at least three times during the cooking time.
5. Remove from the basket and serve with honey.

PB&J WITH BANANAS

Cooking Time: 18 minutes   Serves: 4

Ingredients:
- 8 slices oat nut bread or any whole-grain, oversize bread
- 6 tablespoons peanut butter
- 2 medium bananas, cut into ½-inch-thick slices
- 6 tablespoons pineapple preserves
- ¼ cup coconut, shredded
- ½ cup cornflakes, crushed
- 1 tablespoon olive oil
- 1 egg, beaten

Directions:
1. Combine the shredded coconut, olive oil, and cornflakes in a bowl. Set aside.
2. Rub 1½ tablespoons of peanut butter all over a slice of bread, then place on the banana slices. Brush 1½ tablespoons of preserves over another slice of bread. Assemble the two bread slices to make a sandwich. Repeat with the remaining ingredients.
3. Rub the beaten egg on both sides of the sandwich, then dredge the sandwich into the coconut mixture.
4. Place the well coated sandwich in the basket. Put the air fryer lid on and cook in batches in the preheated instant pot at 350°F for 7 minutes. Flip the sandwich when the lid screen indicates 'TURN FOOD' halfway through, or until lightly browned.
5. Remove from the basket. Cut the sandwich in half to serve.

ALL-IN-ONE HAM TOAST

Cooking Time: 12 minutes   Serves: 1

Ingredients:
- 1 slice bread
- 1 teaspoon butter, softened
- 1 egg
- Salt and freshly ground black pepper, to taste
- 1 tablespoon Cheddar cheese, shredded
- 2 teaspoons ham, diced

Directions:
1. On a cutting board, score a large ½-inch thick hole in the center of the bread slice with a 2½-inch biscuit cutter, or leave a ½-inch space uncut from the hole to the cutting board.
2. Rub the butter all over the bread. Separate the egg in the hole, sprinkle with salt and pepper. Arrange the bread in the air fryer basket.
3. Put the air fryer lid on and cook in the preheated instant pot at 325°F for 5 minutes. Scatter the diced ham and cheese on the top of the bread and cook for 1 minute more.
4. Remove from the basket and serve warm.

BACON AND PEAR ENGLISH MUFFINS WITH PROVOLONE CHEESE

Cooking Time: 15 minutes   Serves: 4 Muffins

Ingredients:
- 2 strips turkey bacon, cut in half crosswise
- ¼ ripe pear, peeled and thinly sliced
- 2 whole-grain English muffins, split in half crosswise
- 4 slices Provolone cheese
- 1 cup fresh baby spinach, long stems removed

Directions:
1. Arrange the bacon in the air fryer basket. Put the air fryer lid on and cook in the preheated instant pot at 400°F for 5 minutes. Flip when the lid screen indicates 'TURN FOOD' halfway through, or until the bacon curls. Transfer to a plate lined with paper towels.
2. Arrange the English muffin halves in the basket and cook at 400°F until golden brown, for about 2 minutes.
3. Open the lid, put a bacon strip, pear slices, a slice of cheese, and baby spinach on each muffin half.
4. Put the lid on and cooking at 350°F for 2 minutes until the cheese melts.
5. Remove the muffins from the basket and serve warm.

TRIAL MIX NUT MUFFINS

Cooking Time: 25 minutes   Serves: 8 Muffins

Ingredients:
- ½ cup whole-wheat flour, plus 2 tablespoons
- 2 tablespoons flaxseed meal
- ½ teaspoon baking soda
- ¼ cup oat bran
- ½ teaspoon baking powder
- ½ teaspoon cinnamon
- ¼ cup brown sugar
- ¼ teaspoon salt
- 1 egg
- ½ cup buttermilk
- ½ teaspoon pure vanilla extract
- 2 tablespoons butter, melted
- ¼ cup walnuts, chopped
- ¼ cup pecans, chopped
- 1 tablespoon sunflower seeds
- 1 tablespoon pumpkin seeds
- ½ cup carrots, grated
- 8 foil muffin cups, liners removed and sprayed with cooking spray

Directions:
1. Combine the flour, flaxseed meal, baking soda, oat bran, baking powder, cinnamon, sugar, and salt in a bowl. Set aside.
2. Whisk together the egg, buttermilk, vanilla, and butter in a separate bowl. Add the flour mixture into the egg mixture. Stir well to mix. Fold in the walnuts, pecans, seeds, and carrots.
3. Divide the mixture among the muffin cups. Arrange the cups in the air fryer basket. You may need to work in batches to avoid overcrowding.
4. Put the air fryer lid on and cook in the preheated instant pot at 325°F for 10 minutes or until tops spring back when touched lightly.
5. Remove the muffins from the basket and serve warm.

OAT BRAN AND DATE MUFFINS

Cooking Time: 20 minutes   Serves: 8 Muffins

Ingredients:
- ½ cup dates, chopped
- ⅔ cup oat bran
- ½ cup flour
- 1 teaspoon baking powder
- ½ teaspoon baking soda
- ¼ cup brown sugar
- ⅛ teaspoon salt
- 1 egg
- ½ cup buttermilk
- 2 tablespoons canola oil
- 8 foil muffin cups, liners removed and sprayed with cooking spray

Directions:
1. Combine the flour, oat bran, baking powder, baking soda, brown sugar, and salt in a bowl.
2. Whisk together the egg, buttermilk, and canola oil in a separate bowl, then pour the egg mixture into the flour mixture. Stir to mix well, then add the chopped dates.
3. Divide the mixture among the muffin cups. Arrange the cups in the air fryer basket. You may need to work in batches to avoid overcrowding.
4. Put the air fryer lid on and cook in the preheated instant pot at 325°F for 10 minutes or until a toothpick inserted in the center comes out clean.
5. Remove the muffins from the basket and serve warm.

EASY BLUEBERRY MUFFINS

Cooking Time: 18 minutes   Serves: 4 Muffins

Ingredients:
- 1 teaspoon blueberry preserves, or other jelly or preserves you like
- 1 cup flour
- 1 teaspoon baking powder
- ½ teaspoon baking soda
- 1 tablespoons sugar
- ¼ teaspoon salt
- 1 egg
- 2 tablespoons butter, melted
- 1 teaspoon pure vanilla extract
- 1 cup buttermilk
- 8 foil muffin cups, liners removed

Directions:
1. Combine the flour, baking powder, baking soda, sugar, and salt in a bowl.
2. Whisk together the egg, butter, vanilla, and buttermilk in a separate bowl.
3. Pour the egg mixture into the flour mixture. Stir to mix well.
4. Use double muffin cups to help muffins hold shape during baking, divide the mixture among the muffins.
5. Arrange the muffins in the air fryer basket, scatter with blueberry preserves. You may need to work in batches to avoid overcrowding.
6. Put the air fryer lid on and bake in the preheated instant pot at 325°F for 8 minutes or until a toothpick inserted in the center comes out clean.
7. Remove the muffins from the basket and serve warm.

LOADED AVOCADO QUESADILLAS

⊕ Cooking Time: 18 minutes   Serves: 4

Ingredients:
- 2 ounces Cheddar cheese, grated
- ½ small avocado, peeled and thinly sliced
- 4 eggs
- 2 tablespoons skim milk
- Salt and freshly ground black pepper, to taste
- 4 flour tortillas
- 4 tablespoons salsa
- Cooking spray

Directions:
1. Whisk the eggs, milk, salt, and pepper together in a bowl.
2. Arrange a 6×6×2-inch baking pan in the air fryer basket, and spritz with cooking spray. Pour the egg mixture into the pan.
3. Put the air fryer lid on and bake in the preheated instant pot at 275°F for 8 minutes. Stir periodically. Transfer to a plate, if using.
4. To make the quesadillas, put the scrambled eggs on half of each piece of tortillas, spread the cheese, salsa, and sliced avocado on top of the eggs. Fold in half.
5. Spritz the basket with cooking spray. Arrange the quesadillas in the basket, and spritz with cooking spray. You may need to work in batches to avoid overcrowding.
6. Put the lid on and cook at 400°F for 2 minutes until the cheese melts and the quesadillas lightly browned.
7. Remove from the basket and cut the quesadillas in half to serve.

BEEF, PORK AND LAMB RECIPES

YUMMY MINI MEATLOAVES WITH TOMATO PUREE

🕐 Cooking Time: 30 minutes   🎩 Serves: 4

Ingredients:
- 2 tablespoons bacon, chopped
- 1 pound ground beef
- 1 garlic clove, minced
- 1 bell pepper, chopped
- 1 small-sized onion, chopped
- ½ teaspoon dried basil
- ½ teaspoon dried marjoram
- ½ teaspoon dried mustard seeds
- Salt and black pepper, to taste
- ½ cup panko crumbs
- 4 tablespoons tomato puree
- Cooking spray

Directions:
1. Put the bacon in a nonstick skillet and cook over moderate heat for 2 minutes. Sprinkle with garlic, bell pepper, and onion. Cook until fragrant, for about 3 minutes. Flip the bacon once during the cooking.
2. Turn the heat off. Fold in the basil, marjoram, mustard seeds, salt, black pepper, panko crumbs, and ground beef. Let stand for a few minutes, then divide and form the mixture into 4 equally-sized mini meatloaves.
3. Use the cooking spray to spritz the air fryer basket. Arrange the meatloaves in the basket, and spritz with the cooking spray.
4. Put the air fryer lid on and cook in the preheated instant pot at 350°F for 20 minutes. Flip the meatloaf when it shows 'TURN FOOD' on the lid screen and pour the tomato puree on top halfway through.
5. Remove the meatloaves from the basket and serve warm.

CRUNCHY VEGGIE AND BEEF SAUSAGES SANDWICHES

Cooking Time: 35 minutes   Serves: 4

Ingredients:
- 4 bell peppers, chopped
- 4 beef sausages
- 2 tablespoons canola oil
- 4 spring onions
- 4 medium-sized tomatoes, halved
- 4 hot dog buns, cut in half crosswise
- 1 tablespoon mustard

Directions:
1. Arrange the bell peppers in the air fryer basket. Brush with 1 tablespoon of canola oil on all sides.
2. Put the air fryer lid on and cook in the preheated instant pot at 375°F for 8 minutes. Shake the basket twice during cooking.
3. Add the spring onions and tomatoes and cook at 350°F for 10 minutes more. Shake the basket twice during cooking. Remove them from the basket and set aside.
4. Place the beef sausages in the air fryer basket. Brush the remaining 1 tablespoon of canola oil over the sausages.
5. Put the lid on and cook at 375°F for 15 minutes. Turn them over when it shows 'TURN FOOD' on the lid screen during the cooking.
6. Divide each sausage between each hot dog bun halves. Serve with mustard and veggies on top.

GRILLED LOIN STEAK WITH WORCESTERSHIRE SAUCE

⊕ Cooking Time: 20 minutes   🎩 Serves: 4

Ingredients:
- 1½ pounds short loin steak
- 2 tablespoons Worcestershire sauce
- 1 tablespoon fresh rosemary, finely chopped
- 1 teaspoon garlic, minced
- 1 cup mayonnaise
- 1 teaspoon smoked paprika
- Sea salt, to taste
- ½ teaspoon ground black pepper

Directions:
1. In a bowl, mix the Worcestershire sauce, rosemary, garlic, mayo, paprika, salt, and pepper. Put the loin steak into this bowl. Toss to coat well. Reserve the mixture.
2. Place the steak in a 6×6×2 inch grill pan. Arrange the pan in the air fryer basket.
3. Put the air fryer lid on and grill in the preheated instant pot at 375°F for 18 minutes. Flip the steak when it shows 'TURN FOOD' on the lid screen halfway through.
4. Serve the steak on a platter with Worcestershire sauce mixture on top.

MEXICAN-STYLE CHEESY BEEF BURRITO

Cooking Time: 20 minutes   Serves: 4

Ingredients:

- 1 pound rump steak
- 1 teaspoon piri piri powder
- 1 teaspoon Mexican oregano
- 1 teaspoon garlic powder
- ½ teaspoon onion powder
- ½ teaspoon cayenne pepper
- Salt and ground black pepper, to taste
- 1 cup Mexican cheese blend
- 4 large whole wheat tortillas
- 1 cup iceberg lettuce, shredded
- Cooking spray

Directions:

1. Sprinkle the steak with piri piri powder, Mexican oregano, garlic powder, onion powder, salt, cayenne pepper, and black pepper in a bowl. Toss to coat well.
2. Slice the steak into strips on a cutting board. Spritz the air fryer basket with cooking spray, then arrange the steak in the air fryer basket.
3. Put the air fryer lid on and cook in the preheated instant pot at 375°F for 12 minutes. Spritz the steak with cooking spray and flip when the lid screen indicates 'TURN FOOD' halfway through.
4. Add the cheese blend on top and cook for an additional 2 minutes until cheese melts.
5. Divide the steak mixture between the wheat tortillas and spread the lettuce on top. Roll the tortillas up to make the burrito and serve warm.

MARINATED TENDER FLANK STEAK

Cooking Time: 20 minutes   Serves: 3

Ingredients:
- 1½ pounds flank steak
- ½ cup red wine
- ½ cup apple cider vinegar
- ½ teaspoon ground black pepper
- ½ teaspoon red pepper flakes, crushed
- ½ teaspoon dried basil
- 1 teaspoon thyme
- 2 tablespoons soy sauce
- Cooking spray

Directions:
1. Add all ingredients except the steak to a large mixing bowl. Whisk together until fully combined.
2. Add the steak in the bowl. Toss to coat well. Wrap the bowl in plastic and let marinate the fridge for at least 1 hour.
3. Discard the marinade. Transfer the steak to a large dish. Pat dry with paper towels.
4. Spritz the air fryer basket with cooking spray. Place the flank steak in the air fryer basket.
5. Put the air fryer lid on and cook in the preheated instant pot at 400°F for 12 minutes. Spritz the steak with cooking spray and flip when it shows 'TURN FOOD' on the lid screen during cooking time.
6. Transfer the steak to a serving dish and serve.

SMOKED VIENNA SAUSAGE WITH GRILLED BROCCOLI

🕐 Cooking Time: 25 minutes   🧢 Serves: 4

Ingredients:
- 1 pound beef Vienna sausage, cut into bite sized pieces
- 1 pound broccoli
- ½ cup mayonnaise
- 1 teaspoon garlic powder
- 1 teaspoon yellow mustard
- ¼ teaspoon black pepper
- 1 tablespoon olive oil
- 1 tablespoon fresh lemon juice
- Cooking spray

Directions:
1. Spritz the air fryer basket with cooking spray. Arrange the sausage pieces in the basket, and spritz with cooking spray.
2. Put the air fryer lid on and cook in the preheated instant pot at 375°F for 15 minutes. Shake the basket periodically.
3. Meanwhile, combine the mayonnaise with the garlic powder, mustard, black pepper, olive oil, and lemon juice, then add the broccoli. Toss to coat well.
4. Remove the sausage from the basket, place the broccoli in the basket. Put the lid on and grill at 400°F for 6 minutes, shaking the basket periodically.
5. Serve the sausage with the grilled broccoli on the side.

FRAGRANT T-BONE STEAK

⏱ Cooking Time: 20 minutes   🎩 Serves: 3

Ingredients:
- 1 pound T-bone steak
- 4 garlic cloves, cut into flakes
- ¼ cup all-purpose flour
- 2 tablespoons olive oil
- 2 heaping tablespoons cilantro, chopped

Sauce:
- ¼ cup tamari sauce
- 4 tablespoons tomato paste
- 1 teaspoon Sriracha sauce
- 2 tablespoons white vinegar
- 2 teaspoons brown sugar
- 1 teaspoon dried rosemary
- ½ teaspoon dried basil

Directions:
1. Evenly spread the garlic flakes on the T-bone steak on a plate.
2. Put the flour in a bowl, then dredge the steak in the flour.
3. Rub the steak with the olive oil and transfer to the air fryer basket.
4. Put the air fry lid on and grill the steak in the preheated instant pot at 400°F for 10 minutes. Flip the steak when the lid screen indicates 'TURN FOOD' halfway through.
5. In the meantime, mix the tamar, tomato paste, Sriracha, white vinegar, brown sugar, rosemary, and basil in a separate bowl.
6. Pour the mixture over the steak. Put the lid on and cook for 5 minutes more.
7. Serve the steak with the fresh cilantro on top.

SAUSAGE SCALLION BALLS WITH TANGY MUSTARD AND PICKLED CUCUMBERS

Cooking Time: 20 minutes   Serves: 4

Ingredients:
- 1½ pounds beef sausage, minced
- 4 tablespoons scallions, chopped
- 4 teaspoons mustard
- 4 pickled cucumbers
- 1 teaspoon Worcestershire sauce
- 1 cup rolled oats
- Salt and freshly milled black pepper, to taste
- 1 teaspoon paprika
- ½ teaspoon garlic, granulated
- 1 teaspoon dried basil
- ½ teaspoon dried oregano
- Cooking spray

Directions:
1. Thoroughly mix the minced sausage meat, Worcestershire sauce, oats, scallions, salt, black pepper, paprika, garlic, basil, and oregano in a bowl.
2. Divide and form the sausage mixture into 4 equally sized meatballs.
3. Spritz the air fryer basket with cooking spray, then arrange the meatballs in the air fryer basket.
4. Put the air fryer lid on and cook in the preheated instant pot at 375°F for 15 minutes. Spritz the meatballs with cooking spray and turn them over when it shows 'TURN FOOD' on the lid screen during cooking time.
5. Serve the meatballs on the platter with mustard and cucumbers.

CRUNCHY STEAK FINGERS WITH ZESTY LIME SAUCE

Cooking Time: 20 minutes   Serves: 4

Ingredients:

- 1½ pounds sirloin steak
- ¼ cup fresh lime juice
- ¼ cup soy sauce
- 1 teaspoon celery seeds
- 1 teaspoon mustard seeds
- 1 teaspoon garlic powder
- 1 teaspoon shallot powder
- Sea salt and black pepper, to taste
- 1 teaspoon red pepper flakes
- 2 eggs
- ¼ cup Parmesan cheese
- 1 teaspoon paprika
- 1 tablespoon olive oil
- 1 cup bread crumbs

Directions:

1. Cut the steak into cubes on a cutting board, pound with a mallet, then cut into finger sized strips about 1-inch.
2. Put the steak strips in a large bowl, then mix with the lime juice, soy sauce, celery seeds, mustard seeds, garlic powder, shallot powder, salt, black pepper, and red pepper flakes. Leave the bowl in the fridge to marinade for 3 hours.
3. Whisk the eggs in a separate bowl. Set aside. Combine the Parmesan cheese, paprika, olive oil, and bread crumbs in a third bowl.
4. Reserve the marinade. Lay the steak in the whisked egg, then dunk into the bread crumb mixture.
5. Arrange the well-coated steak in the air fryer basket. Put the air fryer lid on and cook in the preheated instant pot at 400°F for 14 minutes, flipping when it shows 'TURN FOOD' on the air fryer lid screen during cooking time.
6. Meanwhile, in the saucepan, heat the reserved marinade over medium heat and simmer until perfectly warmed.
7. Serve the steak on a platter with the marinade on the side.

BEEF KOFTA KEBABS SANDWICH

Cooking Time: 30 minutes   Serves: 2

Ingredients:
- 1 pound ground beef chuck
- ½ cup leeks, chopped
- 2 garlic cloves, smashed
- 3 saffron threads
- 2 tablespoons fresh parsley leaves, chopped
- ½ teaspoon ground sumac
- 1 teaspoon cayenne pepper
- A pinch of salt
- ¼ teaspoon ground black pepper
- 4 tablespoons tahini sauce
- 4 slices of warm flat bread, soaked in water until fully tender
- 2 tomatoes, cut into slices
- 4 ounces baby arugula

Directions:
1. Mix together the ground beef meat, chopped leeks, garlic, saffron, parsley, sumac, cayenne pepper, salt, and black pepper.
2. To make the kofta kebabs, shape the beef mixture into two 8-inch cylinder.
3. Arrange the kofta kebabs in the air fryer basket. Put the air fry lid on and cook in the preheated instant pot at 350 °F for 25 minutes. Flip the kofta kebabs when the lid screen indicates 'TURN FOOD' halfway through the cooking time.
4. Assemble the sandwiches by spreading the tahini sauce on a flat bread, topping with a kofta kebab, tomatoes, baby arugula, and another slice of bread. Repeat with the remaining bread slices and kofta kebab.
5. Serve the sandwich on a platter.

GERMANY BEEF SCHNITZEL WITH BUTTERMILK SPAETZLE

Cooking Time: 20 minutes   Serves: 2

Ingredients:
- 2 thin-cut minute steaks
- 1 egg
- 1 teaspoon paprika
- ½ teaspoon ground black pepper
- ½ teaspoon salt
- 1 tablespoon butter, melted
- ½ teaspoon coarse sea salt
- ½ cup tortilla chips, crushed

Buttermilk Spaetzle:
- ½ cup buttermilk
- 1 egg
- ½ cup all-purpose flour
- ½ teaspoon salt
- ½ tablespoon olive oil

Directions:
1. Whisk together the egg, paprika, black pepper, and salt in a shallow bowl. In another bowl, mix in the butter, coarse sea salt, and crushed tortilla chips. Set aside. Pound the steak into ¼-inch thick with a mallet.
2. To make the schnitzel, lay the steak into the egg mixture, then fully coat by rolling in the butter mixture.
3. Arrange the steak in the air fryer basket. Put the air fry lid on and cook in the preheated instant pot at 350°F for 13 minutes. Flip the steak when the lid screen indicates 'TURN FOOD' halfway through the cooking time.
4. Meanwhile, boil a large saucepan of salted water. To make the buttermilk spaetzle, whisk the eggs, flour, buttermilk, and salt in a third bowl.
5. Press the spaetzle mixture down to squeeze out of the holes of a potato ricer into the boiling water.
6. Use a slotted spoon to scoop the spaetzle out after they float and transfer to a bowl of cold water to let them firm up.
7. To keep them from sticking, transfer the spaetzle to a fourth bowl, toss with the olive oil.
8. Remove the schnitzel from the basket and serve with the spaetzle.

HUNGARIAN BEEF SAUSAGE GOULASH

◷ Cooking Time: 40 minutes   🧢 Serves: 2

Ingredients:

- 4 beef good quality sausages, thinly sliced
- 1 tablespoon lard, melted
- 1 bell pepper, chopped
- 2 red chilies, finely chopped
- 1 shallot, chopped
- 1 teaspoon ginger-garlic paste
- Salt and ground black pepper, to taste
- 1 teaspoon smoked paprika
- 1 cup beef bone broth
- ½ cup tomato puree
- 3 handfuls spring greens, shredded

Directions:

1. In a frying pan, melt the lard over medium-high heat, then add and sauté the peppers and shallots for about 4 minutes or until aromatic.
2. Mix in the ginger-garlic paste and cook for one minute more. Sprinkle with salt and black pepper, remove the pan from the heat and set aside.
3. Arrange the sausages in the air fryer basket and cook in batches in the preheated instant pot at 375°F for 8 minutes or until lightly browned, shaking the basket occasionally.
4. Transfer the sausages to a 6×6×2-inch baking pan. Sprinkle with the smoked paprika, pour in the broth and tomato puree. Arrange the pan in the basket.
5. Put the lid on and air fry at 325°F for about 30 minutes. Add the peppers and cook for 5 minutes more or until tender.
6. Remove the pan from the basket. Scatter the spring greens on top. Serve with the hot rice, if desired.

TASTY SAUSAGES IN BREAD PUDDING

⊕Cooking Time: 45 minutes   ◖Serves: 4

Ingredients:
- 6 beef sausages (frozen or fresh)

Batter:
- 1 cup plain flour
- A pinch of salt
- 2 eggs, beaten
- 1 cup semi-skimmed milk
- 1 tablespoon butter, melted

Directions:
1. Cook the sausages in the preheated instant pot at 375°F for 15 minutes until lightly browned. Turn them over when the lid screen indicates 'TURN FOOD' during the cooking time.
2. Meanwhile, to prepare the batter, put the flour into a bowl with salt; make a well in the center of flour. Add the beaten eggs into it. Gently whisk in the milk and butter. Stir all of them until it has a thick consistency. Set aside.
3. Dredge the cooked sausage in the batter to coat well, then put the sausage back to the air fryer basket and cook at 375°F for about 20 minutes. Flip the sausage when the lid screen indicates 'TURN FOOD' halfway through, or until deep golden.
4. Remove the sausage from the air fryer basket and serve.

YOGURT BEEF NUGGETS WITH CHEESY MUSHROOMS

Preparation Time + Cooking Time:25 minutes   Serves: 4

Ingredients:
- 4 tablespoons yogurt
- 1 pound cube steak, cut into bite-size pieces
- 1 cup Swiss cheese, shredded
- 1 pound button mushrooms
- 2 eggs
- 1 cup tortilla chips, crushed
- 1 teaspoon dry mesquite flavored seasoning mix
- Coarse salt and ground black pepper, to taste
- 1 tablespoon olive oil
- ½ teaspoon onion powder
- Cooking spray

Directions:
1. Beat the eggs and yogurt in a bowl. Set aside.
2. Put the tortilla chips, mesquite seasoning, salt, pepper, olive oil, and onion powder in a zip lock bag. Shake to combine.
3. To make the beef nuggets, lay the steak pieces in the egg mixture, then put them in the bag, and shake to coat well.
4. Place the nuggets in the air fryer basket and cook in the preheated instant pot at 400°F for 10 minutes. Turn them over when it shows 'TURN FOOD' on the air fryer lid screen during cooking time.
5. Remove the nuggets from the basket, spritz the basket with cooking spray. Add the mushrooms, then spread with shredded Swiss cheese on top.
6. Put the air fryer lid on and bake in the preheated instant pot at 400°F for 5 minutes.
7. Remove from the basket and serve with the beef nuggets.

ASIAN-STYLE BEEF DUMPLINGS WITH SAVORY SAUCE

⊕Cooking Time: 25 minutes　　　⬛Serves:　5

Ingredients:
- 20 wonton wrappers
- Cooking spray

Filling:
- ½ pound ground beef chuck
- ½ pound beef sausage, chopped
- 1 cup Chinese cabbage, shredded
- 1 bell pepper, chopped
- 1 onion, chopped
- 2 garlic cloves, minced
- 1 medium-sized egg, beaten
- Sea salt and ground black pepper, to taste

Sauce:
- 2 tablespoons soy sauce
- 2 teaspoons sesame oil
- 2 teaspoons sesame seeds, lightly toasted
- 2 tablespoons seasoned rice vinegar
- ½ teaspoon chili sauce

Directions:
1. To make the filling, put the ground chuck, sausage, cabbage, bell pepper, onion, garlic, egg, salt, and black pepper in a mixing bowl and mix them well.
2. To make dumplings, place the wrappers on a clean and lightly floured work surface. Scoop the filling to the center of the wrappers, then fold each wrapper in half and pinch the edges to form a half moon to seal.
3. Spritz the air fryer basket with cooking spray, then arrange the dumplings in the air fryer basket, and spritz with cooking spray.
4. Put the air fryer lid on and cook in the preheated instant pot at 400°F for 10 minutes, flipping when it shows 'TURN FOOD' on the air fryer lid screen during cooking time. .
5. In the meantime, blend the soy sauce, sesame oil, sesame seeds, rice vinegar, and chili sauce together in a bowl.
6. Serve the beef dumplings with the sauce on the side.

PARMESAN PORK CHOPS

⊕Cooking Time: 12 minutes   ⬤Serves: 6

Ingredients:
- Pork chops – 1 1/2 pounds, boneless
- Almond flour – 1/3 cup
- Paprika – 1 tsp.
- Creole seasoning – 1/2 tsp.
- Garlic powder – 1 tsp.
- Parmesan cheese – 1/4 cup, grated

Directions:
Add all ingredients except pork chops into the zip-lock bag. Add pork chops. Seal bag and shake well. Place pork chops into the multi-level air fryer basket and place basket into the instant pot. Seal pot with the air fryer lid. Select air fry mode and cook at 400 F for 12 minutes. Serve.

POULTRY RECIPES

SOY HONEY CHICKEN

⊕Cooking Time: 16 minutes   ⬤Serves: 4

Ingredients:
- Chicken thighs – 1 ½ pounds
- For marinade:
- Ground ginger – ¼ tsp.
- Garlic powder – ½ tsp.
- Honey – 3 tbsps.
- Olive oil – ¼ cup
- Soy sauce – 1/3 cup
- Pepper & salt, to taste

Directions:
Add all marinade ingredients into the large mixing bowl and mix well. Add chicken and coat well. Cover bowl and place in the refrigerator overnight. Remove marinated chicken from marinade and place into the multi-level air fryer basket and place the basket into the instant pot. Seal pot with the air fryer lid. Select air fry mode and cook at 400 F for 16 minutes. Turn chicken halfway through. Serve.

SIMPLE GARLIC BUTTER CHICKEN

⏲ Cooking Time: 16 minutes   🎩 Serves: 4

Ingredients:
- Chicken breasts – 4, boneless
- Garlic powder – ¼ tsp.
- Butter – 2 tbsps., melted
- Black pepper – ¼ tsp.
- Salt – ½ tsp.

Directions:
In a small bowl, mix together butter, garlic powder, black pepper, and salt and rub over chicken breasts. Place chicken breasts into the multi-level air fryer basket and place the basket into the instant pot. Seal pot with the air fryer lid. Select air fry mode and cook at 380 F for 16 minutes. Turn chicken halfway through. Serve.

JUICY CHICKEN BREAST

⏲ Cooking Time: 10 minutes   🎩 Serves: 4

Ingredients:
- Chicken tenderloins – 1 pound
- Greek seasoning – 1 tbsp.
- Olive oil – 2 tbsps.

Directions:
Add chicken, Greek seasoning and olive oil into the large mixing bowl and coat well. Place chicken into the multi-level air fryer basket and place the basket into the instant pot. Seal pot with the air fryer lid. Select air fry mode and cook at 380 F for 10 minutes. Serve.

DELICIOUS TURKEY BURGER PATTIES

⏱ Cooking Time: 12 minutes   🧢 Serves: 4

Ingredients:
- Ground turkey – 1 pound
- Garlic – 1 tsp., minced
- Small onion – 1, diced
- Jalapeno pepper – 1, diced
- Pepper & salt, to taste

Directions:
Add all ingredients into the mixing bowl and mix until thoroughly combined. Make four equal shaped patties and place them into the multi-level air fryer basket and place the basket into the instant pot. Seal pot with the air fryer lid. Select air fry mode and cook at 380 F for 12 minutes. Turn patties halfway through. Serve.

PARMESAN CHICKEN WINGS

⏱ Cooking Time: 30 minutes   🧢 Serves: 4

Ingredients:
- Chicken wings – 1 pound
- Parmesan cheese – ¼ cup, grated
- Butter – 3 tbsps., melted
- Herb & garlic seasoning – ½ tsp.

Directions:
Add chicken wings into the multi-level air fryer basket and place the basket into the instant pot. Seal pot with the air fryer lid. Select air fry mode and cook at 380 F for 30 minutes. Turn chicken wings halfway through. In a mixing bowl, mix together melted butter, cheese, and seasoning. Add cooked chicken wings in a bowl and toss to coat. Serve.

ASIAN CHICKEN WINGS

⊕Cooking Time: 25 minutes   Serves: 4

Ingredients:
- Chicken wings – 1 pound
- Garlic powder – 1 tbsp.
- Brown sugar – ½ cup
- Soy sauce – ½ cup

Directions:
In a small saucepan, add garlic powder, brown sugar, and soy sauce and bring to boil. Stir constantly because it will burn quickly. In a large bowl, add chicken wings. Pour sauce over chicken wings and coat well. Cover bowl and place in the refrigerator for 30 minutes. Add marinated chicken wings into a multi-level air fryer basket and place the basket into the instant pot. Seal pot with the air fryer lid. Select air fry mode and cook at 360 F for 25 minutes. Turn chicken wings after 10 minutes. Serve.

TASTY SESAME CHICKEN

⊕Cooking Time: 30 minutes   Serves: 2

Ingredients:
- Chicken breasts – 2, boneless
- Onion powder – 1 tbsp.
- Garlic powder – 1 tbsp.
- Paprika – 1 tbsp.
- Sesame oil – 2 tbsps.
- Black pepper – ½ tsp.
- Kosher salt – 1 tsp.

Directions:
In a small bowl, mix together onion powder, garlic powder, paprika, oil, pepper, and salt and rub all over chicken breasts. Place chicken breasts into the multi-level air fryer basket and place the basket into the instant pot. Seal pot with the air fryer lid. Select air fry mode and cook at 380 F for 30 minutes. Turn chicken after 20 minutes. Serve.

FLAVORFUL TANDOORI CHICKEN THIGHS

⏲ Cooking Time: 30 minutes   🧢 Serves: 4

Ingredients:
- Chicken thighs – 1 pound
- For marinade:
- Ground turmeric – ½ tsp.
- Chili powder – 1 tsp.
- Ground cumin – 2 tsps.
- Vinegar – ¼ cup
- Ginger garlic paste – 2 tbsps.
- Yogurt – 1 cup
- Salt – ½ tsp.

Directions:
Add all marinade ingredients into the large mixing bowl and mix well. Add chicken and coat thoroughly. Cover bowl and place in the refrigerator for 1 hour. Remove chicken from marinade and place in a multi-level air fryer basket and place the basket into the instant pot. Seal pot with the air fryer lid. Select air fry mode and cook at 350 F for 30 minutes. Turn chicken halfway through. Serve.

SPICY HASSELBACK CHICKEN

⏲ Cooking Time: 16 minutes   🧢 Serves: 2

Ingredients:
- Chicken breasts – 2, skinless & boneless
- Cheddar cheese – ½ cup, shredded
- Pickled jalapenos – ¼ cup, chopped
- Cream cheese – 2 oz
- Bacon slices – 4, cooked and crumbled

Directions:
In a bowl, mix together ¼ cup cheddar cheese, cream cheese, jalapenos, and bacon and set aside. Using a sharp knife make six slits on top of chicken breasts. Stuff cheese mixture into the slits. Place chicken into the multi-level air fryer

basket and place basket into the instant pot. Seal pot with the air fryer lid. Select air fry mode and cook at 350 F for 15 minutes. Top with remaining cheese and air fry for 1 minute. Serve.

SOUTHERN CHICKEN THIGHS

⊕ Cooking Time: 20 minutes   ⬤ Serves: 4

Ingredients:
- Chicken thighs – 4
- Southern seasoning – 1 1/2 tbsps.

Directions:
Rub chicken thighs with southern seasoning. Place chicken thighs into the multi-level air fryer basket and place the basket into the instant pot. Seal pot with the air fryer lid. Select air fry mode and cook at 360 F for 20 minutes. Turn chicken halfway through. Serve.

AIR FRYER TURKEY BREAST

⊕ Cooking Time: 40 minutes   ⬤ Serves: 3

Ingredients:
- Turkey breast – 1 pound
- Fresh rosemary – 1 tsp., chopped
- Fresh thyme – 1 tsp., chopped
- Garlic clove – 1, minced
- Butter – 4 tbsps., melted
- Pepper & salt, to taste

Directions:
In a small bowl, mix together melted butter, garlic, thyme, rosemary, pepper, and salt and brush all over turkey breast. Place turkey breast into the multi-level air fryer basket and place the basket into the instant pot. Seal pot with the air fryer lid. Select air fry mode and cook at 375 F for 40 minutes. Slice and serve.

JUICY TURKEY PATTIES

🕐 Cooking Time: 16 minutes   🧢 Serves: 4

Ingredients:
- Ground turkey – 1 pound
- Breadcrumbs – ¼ cup
- Garlic – 1 tsp., minced
- Worcestershire sauce – 2 tsps.
- Ranch seasoning – 1 tbsp.
- Onion – ½, minced
- Apple sauce – ¼ cup
- Pepper & salt, to taste

Directions:
Add all ingredients into the mixing bowl and mix until combined thoroughly. Make patties and place them in the refrigerator for 30 minutes. Remove turkey patties from the refrigerator and place them into the multi-level air fryer basket. Place the basket into the instant pot. Seal pot with the air fryer lid. Select air fry mode and cook at 360 F for 16 minutes. Turn patties halfway through. Serve.

FISH AND SEAFOOD RECIPES

LEMON PEPPER WHITE FISH FILLETS

Cooking Time: 10 minutes   Serves: 2

Ingredients:
- White fish fillets – 12 oz
- Onion powder – 1/2 tsp.
- Lemon pepper seasoning – 1/2 tsp.
- Garlic powder – 1/2 tsp.
- Olive oil – 1 tbsp.
- Pepper & salt, to taste

Directions:
Brush fish fillets with olive oil and season with onion powder, lemon pepper seasoning, garlic powder, pepper, and salt. Place fish fillets into the multi-level air fryer basket and place the basket into the instant pot. Seal pot with the air fryer lid. Select air fry mode and cook at 360 F for 10 minutes. Serve.

QUICK & EASY SALMON

Cooking Time: 10 minutes   Serves: 2

Ingredients:
- Salmon fillets – 2, skinless and boneless
- Olive oil – 1 tsp.
- Pepper & salt, to taste

Directions:
Brush salmon fillets with oil and season with pepper and salt. Place salmon fillets into the multi-level air fryer basket and place the basket into the instant pot. Seal pot with the air fryer lid. Select air fry mode and cook at 360 F for 10 minutes. Serve.

HEALTHY TUNA PATTIES

Cooking Time: 10 minutes   Serves: 2

Ingredients:
- Cans of tuna – 2
- Lemon juice – 1/2
- Onion powder – 1/2 tsp.
- Garlic powder – 1 tsp.
- Mayonnaise – 1 1/2 tbsps.
- Almond flour – 1 1/2 tbsps.
- Pepper – 1/4 tsp.
- Dried dill – 1/2 tsp.
- Salt – 1/4 tsp.

Directions:
Add all ingredients in a mixing bowl and mix until thoroughly combined. Make four patties from the mixture and place into the multi-level air fryer basket and place the basket into the instant pot. Seal pot with the air fryer lid. Select air fry mode and cook at 400 F for 10 minutes. Serve.

DELICIOUS SCALLOPS

Cooking Time: 7 minutes   Serves: 4

Ingredients:
- Scallops – 1 pound
- Basil pesto – 1/4 cup
- Olive oil – 1 tbsp.
- Garlic – 2 tsps., minced
- Heavy cream – 3 tbsps.
- Pepper & salt, to taste

Directions:
Season scallops with pepper and salt and add into the multi-level air fryer basket and place the basket into the instant pot. Seal pot with the air fryer lid. Select air fry mode and cook at 320 F for 6 minutes. Turn scallops halfway through. Meanwhile, in a small saucepan, heat oil over medium heat. Add garlic and sauté for 30 seconds. Add heavy cream and pesto and cook for 2 minutes. Remove saucepan from heat. Add scallops into the large bowl. Pour pesto sauce over scallops and toss well. Serve.

OLD BAY SEASONED TILAPIA

Cooking Time: 7 minutes   Serves: 2

Ingredients:
- Tilapia fillets – 2
- Old bay seasoning – 1/2 tsp.
- Lemon pepper – 1/4 tsp.
- Butter – 1/2 tbsp., melted
- Salt

Directions:
Brush fish fillets with butter and season with old bay seasoning, lemon pepper, and salt. Place fish fillets into the multi-level air fryer basket and place the basket into the instant pot. Seal pot with the air fryer lid. Select air fry mode and cook at 400 F for 7 minutes. Serve.

SPICED PRAWNS

Cooking Time: 6 minutes   Serves: 2

Ingredients:
- Prawns – 6
- Chili flakes – 1 tsp.
- Chili powder – 1/2 tsp.
- Black pepper – 1/4 tsp.
- Salt – 1/4 tsp.

Directions:
In a bowl, place prawns, chili powder, pepper, chili flakes, and salt into the bowl and toss well. Add prawns into the multi-level air fryer basket and place the basket into the instant pot. Seal pot with the air fryer lid. Select air fry mode and cook at 350 F for 6 minutes. Serve.

CAYENNE PEPPER SHRIMP

⏲ Cooking Time: 6 minutes   🧢 Serves: 2

Ingredients:
- Shrimp – 1/2 pound, peeled and deveined
- Olive oil – 1 tbsp.
- Paprika – 1/4 tsp.
- Old bay seasoning – 1/2 tsp.
- Cayenne pepper – 1/4 tsp.
- Salt – 1/8 tsp.

Directions:
Add all ingredients into the mixing bowl and toss well. Add shrimp into the multi-level air fryer basket and place the basket into the instant pot. Seal pot with the air fryer lid. Select air fry mode and cook at 390 F for 6 minutes. Serve.

CATFISH FISH FILLETS

⏲ Cooking Time: 20 minutes   🧢 Serves: 3

Ingredients:
- Catfish fillets – 3
- Fresh parsley – 1 tbsp., chopped
- Olive oil – 1 tbsp.
- Fish seasoning – 1/4 cup

Directions:
Season fish fillets with seasoning and place into a multi-level air fryer basket and place the basket into the instant pot. Seal pot with the air fryer lid. Select air fry mode and cook at 400 F for 20 minutes. Turn fish fillets halfway through. Garnish with parsley. Serve.

COCONUT SHRIMP

⊕ Cooking Time: 5 minutes   Serves: 2

___

Ingredients:
- Shrimp – 8 oz, peeled
- Cayenne pepper – 1/8 tsp.
- Shredded coconut – 1/4 cup
- Almond flour – 1/4 cup
- Egg whites – 2
- Salt – 1/4 tsp.

Directions:
Whisk egg whites in a shallow bowl. In a separate shallow dish, mix together the shredded coconut, almond flour, and cayenne pepper. Dip shrimp into the egg mixture then coat with coconut mixture and place it into the multi-level air fryer basket and place the basket into the instant pot. Seal pot with the air fryer lid. Select air fry mode and cook at 400 F for 5 minutes. Serve.

PARMESAN SHRIMP

⊕ Cooking Time: 10 minutes   Serves: 3

___

Ingredients:
- Shrimp –, 1 pound, peeled and deveined
- Oregano – 1/4 tsp.
- Pepper – 1/2 tsp.
- Parmesan cheese – 1/4 cup, grated
- Garlic cloves – 3, minced
- Olive oil – 1 tbsp.
- Onion powder – 1/2 tsp.
- Basil – 1/2 tsp.

Directions:
Add all ingredients into the large bowl and toss well. Add shrimp into the multi-level air fryer basket and place the basket into the instant pot. Seal pot with the air fryer lid. Select air fry mode and cook at 350 F for 10 minutes. Serve.

SIMPLE TUNA PATTIES

Cooking Time: 6 minutes   Serves: 4

Ingredients:
- Egg – 1, lightly beaten
- Breadcrumbs – 1/4 cup
- Mustard – 1 tbsp.
- Can tuna – 7 oz, drained
- Pepper & salt, to taste

Directions:
Add all ingredients into the mixing bowl and mix until thoroughly combined.
Make four patties from the mixture and place into the multi-level air fryer basket
and place the basket into the instant pot. Seal pot with the air fryer lid. Select air
fry mode and cook at 400 F for 6 minutes. Turn patties halfway through. Serve.

SALMON DILL PATTIES

Cooking Time: 10 minutes   Serves: 4

Ingredients:
- Can salmon – 15 oz, drained and remove bones
- Dill – 1 tsp., chopped
- Breadcrumbs – 1/2 cup
- Onion – 1/4 cup, chopped
- Egg – 1, lightly beaten
- Pepper & salt, to taste

Directions:
Add all ingredients into the mixing bowl and mix until thoroughly combined.
Make four patties from the mixture and place into the multi-level air fryer basket
and place the basket into the instant pot. Seal pot with the air fryer lid. Select air

fry mode and cook at 370 F for 10 minutes. Turn patties halfway through. Serve.

FLAVORFUL TILAPIA

Cooking Time: 8 minutes   Serves: 4

Ingredients:
- Tilapia fillets – 2
- Dried oregano – 1 tsp.
- Brown sugar – 2 tsps.
- Paprika – 2 tbsps.
- Cayenne – 1/4 tsp.
- Cumin – 1/2 tsp.
- Garlic powder – 1 tsp.
- Salt

Directions:

In a small bowl, mix together cayenne, cumin, garlic powder, oregano, sugar, paprika, and salt and rub all over tilapia fillets. Place tilapia fillets into the multi-level air fryer basket and place the basket into the instant pot. Seal pot with the air fryer lid. Select air fry mode and cook at 400 F for 8 minutes. Turn fish fillets halfway through. Serve.

TANDOORI SALMON WITH VEGETABLES

🕐 Cooking Time: 25 minutes   🧢 Serves: 4

Ingredients:

- 10 ounces salmon, cut into 12 cubes
- ½ tablespoon tandoori spice powder
- 3 cups plain yogurt
- 1 teaspoon green chilli, minced
- 30 leaves fresh mint, chopped
- ½ teaspoon ground cumin
- Salt and pepper to taste
- ½ cucumber, peel, deseeded and diced
- 1 small tomato, peeled, deseeded and diced
- ½ red onion, peel and finely chopped
- Cooking spray

Directions:

1. In a medium bowl, place the tandoori spice powder. Add the salmon cubes into the powder, and toss to coat well. Set aside.
2. In a large bowl, combine ¼ of the yogurt with the chilli, mint, cumin, salt, and pepper. Stir well. Cover the bowl with plastic wrap and place in the refrigerator until ready to use.
3. Place the salmon cubes in the air fryer basket and spritz with cooking spray.
4. Put the air fryer lid on and cook in the preheated instant pot at 390°F for 8 minutes.
5. Meanwhile, mix the remaining yogurt, diced cucumber, tomato, and onion into the prepared yogurt mixture. Stir until well combined, then transfer to a plate.
6. Remove the salmon cubes from the basket. Put them on the yogurt mixture in the plate. Serve warm.

AROMATIC SHRIMP FAJITAS

🕐 Cooking Time: 30 minutes   🎩 Serves: 4

Ingredients:
- 1 pound uncooked medium shrimp, peeled and deveined
- 1 (1.12-ounce) package fajita seasoning mix
- 3 tablespoons olive oil,
- 1 red onion, sliced into thin strips
- 1 red bell pepper, sliced into thin strips
- 1 green bell pepper, sliced into thin strips
- 4 (10-inch) flour tortillas, toasted

Directions:
1. In a bowl, place the shrimp. Sprinkle with 2 teaspoons of the fajita seasoning mix, and drizzle 1 tablespoon of the olive oil over the shrimp. Stir until the shrimp is coated evenly. Set aside.
2. In a large bowl, place the onion and bell peppers. Add in the remaining fajita seasoning mix, and stir well. Pour in 2 tablespoons of the olive oil, and toss to coat well.
3. Place the onion and bell peppers in the air fryer basket. Put the air fryer lid on and cook in the preheated instant pot at 400°F for 12 minutes, stirring once halfway through the cooking, or until tender.
4. Remove the vegetables from the basket to a platter. Set aside and keep warm.
5. Lay the shrimp in the basket and put the lid on. Cook at 400°F for 8 minutes. Flip the shrimp when the lid indicates 'TURN FOOD' halfway through the cooking.
6. On a clean work surface, arrange the tortillas. Evenly spread the vegetables onto each tortilla, then place the shrimp on top.
7. Garnish with the chopped parsley, if desired.

VEGETABLES AND VEGAN RECIPES

RUSTIC SMOKED HALIBUT BRIOCHE

Cooking Time: 25 minutes   Serves: 4

Ingredients:
- 1 pound smoked halibut, chopped
- 4 brioche rolls
- 4 eggs
- 1 teaspoon dried basil
- 1 teaspoon dried thyme
- Salt and black pepper, to taste
- Nonstick cooking spray

Directions:
1. Halve each brioche roll crosswise and use a spoon to hollow out the insides.
2. Spritz the air fryer basket with the nonstick cooking spray. Arrange the brioche in the air fryer basket, and spritz with the nonstick cooking spray.
3. Separate an egg into each brioche hollow. Top with chopped smoked halibut and season with basil, thyme, salt, and pepper.
4. Put the air fryer lid on and bake in the preheated instant pot at 325°F for 20 minutes.
5. Serve the brioche on a plate.

GARLICKY CRAB PATTIES

⏱Cooking Time: 20 minutes   🧢Serves: 3

Ingredients:
- 10 ounces crab meat
- 2 garlic cloves, crushed
- 2 eggs, beaten
- 1 shallot, chopped
- 1 tablespoon olive oil
- 1 teaspoon yellow mustard
- 1 teaspoon fresh cilantro, chopped
- 1 cup tortilla chips, crushed
- ½ teaspoon cayenne pepper
- ½ teaspoon ground black pepper
- Sea salt, to taste
- ¾ cup fresh bread crumbs
- Cooking spray

Directions:
1. In a large bowl, combine the eggs, shallot, garlic, olive oil, mustard, cilantro, crab, tortilla chips, cayenne, pepper, and salt.
2. Divide and form the mixture into 6 equal sized patties. Dredge the patties in a bowl of bread crumbs to coat well. Cover in plastic wrap and refrigerate for 2 hours.
3. Arrange the crab patties in the air fryer basket, spritz with cooking spray.
4. Put the air fryer lid on and cook in the preheated instant pot at 350°F for 14 minutes. Flip the patties when the lid screen indicates 'TURN FOOD' halfway through.
5. Serve the patties on a platter.

COCONUT AND ORANGE JUICY SHRIMP

⏲ Cooking Time: 30 minutes   🧢 Serves: 3

Ingredients:
- 1 pound shrimp, cleaned and deveined
- Sea salt and white pepper, to taste
- ½ cup all-purpose flour
- 1 egg
- 3/2 cup fresh bread crumbs
- ¼ cup unsweetened coconut, shredded
- 2 tablespoons olive oil
- 1 lemon, cut into wedges

Dipping Sauce:
- 2 tablespoons butter
- ½ cup orange juice
- ½ teaspoon tapioca starch
- 2 tablespoons soy sauce
- A pinch of salt
- 2 tablespoons fresh parsley, minced

Directions:
1. On a clean work surface, sprinkle the shrimp with salt and white pepper.
2. Put the flour in a large bowl. Beat the egg in a second bowl. Combine the bread crumbs and coconut in a third bowl.
3. Dredge the shrimp in the flour, then in the beaten egg, then in the coconut mixture to coat well. Cover in plastic wrap and refrigerate for an hour.
4. Arrange the shrimp in the air fryer basket. Drizzle with the olive oil. Put the air fryer lid on and cook in batches in the preheated instant pot at 375°F for 6 minutes.
5. In the meantime, to make the dipping sauce, put the butter in a saucepan and melt over medium-high heat. Stir in the orange juice and bring to a boil. Turn the heat down and simmer for about 7 minutes.
6. Add the tapioca, soy sauce, and salt to the sauce. Continue simmering until the sauce reduced by one third or has thick consistency.
7. Serve the shrimp with the sauce on top along with parsley and lemon wedges.

BEERY HOKI FILLETS WITH DIJON MUSTARD SAUCE

Cooking Time: 20 minutes   Serves: 2

Ingredients:
- 1 bottle (12-ounce) beer
- ½ pound hoki fillets
- 1 teaspoon Dijon mustard
- 1 egg
- 1 teaspoon paprika
- ½ cup flour
- 1 tablespoon fresh lemon juice
- ¼ cup mayonnaise
- 1 teaspoon sweet pickle relish
- ½ teaspoon honey
- Sea salt and black pepper, to taste
- Nonstick cooking spray

Directions:
1. In a mixing bowl, whisk together the egg, paprika and flour, then fold in the beer to make a batter. Dredge the hoki fillets in the batter.
2. Spritz the air fryer basket with cooking spray and arrange the fillets in the air fryer basket.
3. Put the air fryer lid on and cook in the preheated instant pot at 375°F for 12 minutes. Flip the fillets when the lid screen indicates 'TURN FOOD' halfway through.
4. Meanwhile, combine the mustard, lemon juice, mayonnaise, relish honey, salt, and pepper. Cover in plastic wrap and refrigerate the sauce until ready to serve.
5. Serve the fillets warm with the sauce on top.

THAI HALIBUT STEAKS

Cooking Time: 15 minutes   Serves: 2

Ingredients:
- 2 halibut steaks
- 2 tablespoons tamari sauce
- 2 tablespoons fresh lime juice
- 2 tablespoons olive oil
- 1 teaspoon Thai curry paste
- ½-inch lemongrass, finely chopped
- 1 teaspoon basil
- 2 cloves garlic, minced
- 2 tablespoons shallot, minced
- Sea salt and ground black pepper, to taste
- Nonstick cooking spray

Directions:
1. In a large bowl, combine the tamari, lime juice, olive oil, curry paste, lemongrass, basil, garlic, shallot, salt, and pepper. Add the halibut steaks to the mixture. Cover in plastic wrap and marinate for 30 minutes.
2. Spritz the air fryer basket with the nonstick cooking spray. Arrange the halibut steaks in the basket. Reserve the marinade.
3. Put the air fryer lid on and bake in the preheated instant pot at 375°F for 11 to 12 minutes. When the lid screen indicates 'TURN FOOD', flip the halibut steaks.
4. Serve the halibut steaks with the marinade on top.

FRENCH FLAVOR SEA BASS WITH GHERKINS SAUCE

🕐 Cooking Time: 15 minutes   🎩 Serves: 2

Ingredients:
- 2 sea bass fillets
- 1 tablespoon olive oil

Gherkin Sauce:
- 1 tablespoon gherkins, drained and chopped
- 2 tablespoons scallions, finely chopped
- ½ cup mayonnaise
- 2 tablespoons lemon juice
- 1 tablespoon capers, drained and chopped

Directions:
1. Arrange the sea bass fillets on a clean work surface. Rub with olive oil on both sides. Arrange the fillets in the air fryer basket.
2. Put the air fryer lid on and cook in preheated instant pot at 375°F for 8 minutes or until opaque. Flip the fillets when the screen indicates 'TURN FOOD' halfway through.
3. In the meantime, to make the gherkin sauce, combine the gherkins, scallions, mayonnaise, lemon juice, and capers in a small bowl. Cover in plastic wrap and refrigerate to marinate until ready to serve.
4. Remove the cooked sea bass fillets from the basket to a large dish, and serve with the gherkin sauce on top.

JAMAICAN SOLE FRITTERS

Cooking Time: 30 minutes   Serves: 2

Ingredients:
- ½ pound sole fillets
- ½ teaspoon paprika
- ½ cup red onion, chopped
- ½ pound potatoes, mashed
- ½ teaspoon scotch bonnet pepper, minced
- 1 egg, well beaten
- 1 tablespoon olive oil
- 1 bell pepper, finely chopped
- 1 tablespoon coconut aminos
- 2 garlic cloves, minced
- 2 tablespoons fresh parsley, chopped
- Salt and white pepper, to taste
- Nonstick cooking spray

Directions:
1. Spritz the air fryer basket with the nonstick cooking spray.
2. Arrange the sole fillets in the air fryer basket. Put the air fryer lid on and cook in the preheated instant pot at 375°F for 8 minutes. Flip them when the lid screen indicates 'TURN FOOD' halfway through.
3. To make fritters, flake the cooked sole fillets into a bowl. Stir in the paprika, onion, mashed potatoes, scotch bonnet pepper, beaten egg, olive oil, bell pepper, coconut aminos, garlic, parsley, salt, and pepper. Form the mixture into 2 equally sized patties.
4. Arrange the patties in the air fryer basket. Put the air fryer lid on and bake in the preheated instant pot at 375°F for 12 minutes. Flip the patties when the lid screen indicates 'TURN FOOD'.
5. Remove the fried patties (fritters) from the air fryer basket and serve warm.

TILAPIA FILLETS WITH BIRD'S EYE CHILI SAUCE

Cooking Time: 20 minutes   Serves: 2

Ingredients:
- 1 pound tilapia
- ½ Thai Bird's Eye chili, deseeded and finely chopped
- 2 tablespoons lime juice
- 1 teaspoon turmeric powder
- ½ teaspoon ginger powder
- 1 cup coconut milk
- 2 tablespoons Shoyu sauce
- Salt and white pepper, to taste
- Nonstick cooking spray

Directions:
1. Combine the lime juice, turmeric, chili pepper, ginger, coconut milk, shoyu, salt, and pepper in a bowl. Add the tilapia, cover in plastic wrap and marinate for an hour.
2. Spritz the air fryer basket with the nonstick cooking spray. Arrange the marinated tilapia in the air fryer basket. You may need to cook in batches to avoid overcrowding.
3. Put the air fryer lid on and cook in the preheated instant pot at 375°F for 6 minutes. Flip the fish when the lid screen indicates 'TURN FOOD'.
4. Remove the tilapia fillets from the air fryer basket and serve with lime wedges, if desired.

CHEESY HAKE FILLETS CASSEROLE

Cooking Time: 30 minutes   Serves: 4

Ingredients:
- 1 pound hake fillets
- ½ cup Swiss cheese, shredded
- ½ cup Cottage cheese
- 1 tablespoon avocado oil
- Sea salt and ground white pepper, to taste
- 1 teaspoon garlic powder
- 1 bell pepper, deseeded and chopped
- 2 tablespoons shallots, chopped
- ½ cup sour cream
- 1 teaspoon yellow mustard
- 1 tablespoon lime juice
- 1 egg, beaten

Directions:
1. In a 6-inch casserole dish, coat the hake fillets with avocado oil. Season with salt, pepper, and garlic powder. Toss in the bell pepper and chopped shallots.
2. In a separated bowl, combine the sour cream, mustard, lime juice, egg and cottage cheese. Spread the sour cream mixture over the fillets.
3. Arrange the casserole dish in the air fryer basket. Put the air fryer lid on and cook in the preheated instant pot at 375°F for 10 minutes.
4. Sprinkle with the shredded Swiss cheese on top and cook for 7 minutes more.
5. Remove the casserole dish from the basket. Cool for 10 minutes before serving.

BEERY SCALLOPS WITH ROSEMARY

Cooking Time: 10 minutes   Serves: 4

Ingredients:
- 2 pounds sea scallops
- ½ cup beer
- 2 sprigs rosemary, only leaves
- 4 tablespoons butter
- Sea salt and freshly cracked black pepper, to taste

Directions:
1. Combine the sea scallops with beer in a mixing bowl. Cover in plastic wrap and marinate for one hour.
2. In a small bowl, combine the rosemary leaves and melted butter.
3. Arrange the marinated scallops in the air fryer basket. Sprinkle with salt and black pepper. You may need to work in batches to avoid overcrowding.
4. Put the air fryer lid on and cook in batches in the preheated instant pot at 375°F for 9 minutes. Shake the air fryer basket and top the scallops with rosemary-butter mixture when the lid screen indicates 'TURN FOOD' halfway through.
5. Remove the scallops from the air fryer basket and serve.

CHERRY TOMATOES AND JUMBO SHRIMP SKEWERS

⏱ Cooking Time: 30 minutes   🧢 Serves: 4

Ingredients:

- 1 pound cherry tomatoes
- 1½ pounds jumbo shrimp, cleaned, shelled and deveined
- ½ teaspoon marjoram
- ½ teaspoon dried basil
- ½ teaspoon dried oregano
- ½ teaspoon mustard seeds
- 1 tablespoons Sriracha sauce
- 1 teaspoon dried parsley flakes
- 2 tablespoons butter, melted
- Sea salt and ground black pepper, to taste
- 4 wooden skewers, soaked for 15 minutes

Directions:

1. In a large bowl, combine the marjoram, basil, oregano, mustard seeds, Sriracha, parsley, butter, salt, and pepper. Add the cherry tomatoes and shrimp. Toss to coat well.
2. Thread the shrimp and tomatoes on the skewers alternately.
3. Arrange the shrimp skewers in the air fryer basket. You may need to work in batches to avoid overcrowding.
4. Put the air fryer lid on and cook in the preheated instant pot at 375°F for 7 minutes. Flip the shrimp skewers when the lid screen indicates 'TURN FOOD' halfway through.
5. Remove the shrimp skewers from the air fryer basket and serve.

LEMONY SNAPPER FILLETS WITH COCONUT SAUCE

⏱ Cooking Time: 20min /　　🧢 Serves:　2

Ingredients:
- 2 snapper fillets
- 2 tablespoons lemon juice
- ½ cup full-fat coconut milk
- 1 teaspoon fresh ginger, grated
- 1 tablespoon olive oil
- 1 tablespoon cornstarch
- Salt and white pepper, to taste

Directions:
1. In a large bowl, combine the snapper fillets with the lemon juice, coconut milk and ginger. Cover in plastic warp and marinate for one hour.
2. Arrange the fillets in the air fryer basket. Reserve the marinade. Brush the fillets with olive oil on all sides.
3. Put the air fryer lid on and cook in the preheated instant pot at 375°F for 17 minutes. Flip the fillets when the lid screen indicates 'TURN FOOD' halfway through the cooking time.
4. In the meantime, add the marinade in a saucepan and bring to a boil over medium-high heat, stirring constantly.
5. Stir the cornstarch, salt, and pepper into the sauce, lower the heat and simmer for 12 minutes.
6. Serve the snapper fillets with the warm sauce on a plate.

CRAB BRUSCHETTA WITH MOZZARELLA CHEESE

⏱ Cooking Time: 15 minutes   🧢 Serves: 2

Ingredients:
- 8 ounces lump crab meat
- 4 tablespoons mozzarella cheese, crumbled
- 4 slices sourdough bread
- 4 tablespoons mayonnaise
- 2 tablespoons shallots, chopped
- 2 tablespoons ketchup
- 1 teaspoon fresh rosemary, chopped
- 1 teaspoon granulated garlic

Directions:
1. In a large bowl, combine the mayonnaise, crab meat, shallots, ketchup, rosemary and garlic in a bowl. Set aside.
2. To make the bruschetta, place the sourdough bread slices on the clean work surface. Divide the crab mixture between the slices of bread. Sprinkle with mozzarella cheese.
3. Arrange the bruschetta in the air fryer basket. Put the air fryer lid on and bake in the preheated instant pot at 375°F for 10 minutes.
4. Remove the bruschetta from the air fryer basket and serve warm.

MEXICAN STYLE SHRIMP NACHOS WITH SOUR CREAM

Cooking Time: 15 minutes   Serves: 4

Ingredients:
- 1 pound shrimp, cleaned and deveined
- ½ cup sour cream
- 2 tablespoons fresh lemon juice
- ¼ teaspoon cumin powder
- ½ teaspoon garlic powder
- 1 tablespoon olive oil
- 1 teaspoon paprika
- ½ teaspoon shallot powder
- Coarse sea salt and ground black pepper, to taste
- 1 bag (9-ounce) corn tortilla chips
- ¼ cup pickled jalapeño, minced
- 1 cup Pepper Jack cheese, grated

Directions:
1. In a large bowl, toss the shrimp with the lemon juice, cumin, garlic, olive oil, paprika, shallot powder, salt, and pepper.
2. Arrange the well coated shrimp in the air fryer basket. Put the air fryer lid on and cook in the preheated instant pot at 375°F for 7 minutes. Remove the shrimp from the basket.
3. To make shrimp nachos, line the air fryer basket with aluminum foil. Arrange the tortilla chips in the air fryer basket. Top with the shrimp, jalapeño, and cheese.
4. Put the air fryer lid on and cook until the cheese melts, about 2 minutes.
5. Remove the nachos from the air fryer basket and serve with sour cream on top.

BEERY TUNA FRITTERS WITH CHEESE SAUCE

⏱ Cooking Time: 20 minutes   🧢 Serves: 4

Ingredients:
- 1 pound canned tuna, drained
- 1 egg
- 2 tablespoons shallots, minced
- 1 cup bread crumbs
- 1 garlic clove, minced
- Sea salt and ground black pepper, to taste
- 1 tablespoon sesame oil

Sauce:
- 1 cup beer
- 2 tablespoons Colby cheese, grated
- 1 tablespoon rice flour
- 1 tablespoon butter

Directions:
1. In a large bowl, whisk together the egg, shallots, tuna, bread crumbs, garlic, salt, and pepper until it has a thick, even consistency.
2. To make fritters, from the mixture into four equally sized patties. Reserve the patties in the fridge for 2 hours.
3. Coat the patties with sesame oil and place in the air fryer basket. Put the air fryer lid on and cook in the preheated instant pot at 350°F for 14 minutes. Flip the patties when the lid screen indicates 'TURN FOOD' halfway through.
4. Meanwhile, to make the sauce, in a saucepan, melt the butter over moderate heat. As it melts, fold in the flour and beer and stir until frothy.
5. Stir the grated cheese into the sauce and cook until melted, for about 3 to 4 minutes.
6. Top the crisp patties (fritters) with the cheese sauce and serve warm.

GOLDEN POP TARTS WITH STRAWBERRY JAM

Cooking Time: 45 minutes   Serves: 8

Ingredients:
- 1 box (14 ounces) refrigerated pie crust
- 1 cup strawberries, sliced
- 1 teaspoon maple syrup
- 1 tablespoon fresh lemon juice
- 2 tablespoons chia seeds
- ½ cup powdered sugar
- 1 egg, whisked with 1 tablespoon of water (egg wash)

Directions:
1. Place the strawberry slices in a saucepan and heat until caramelized, then add the maple syrup and lemon juice. Keep stirring until fully mixed.
2. Turn off the heat and mix in chia seeds. Cool for 30 minutes until it has a thick consistency. Set aside.
3. On a clean work surface, roll out the pie crusts and cut into equal-sized rectangles.
4. To make the pop tarts, place a spoon of strawberry jam on one piece of rectangular crust, then put on your second piece of crust. Repeat with remaining crusts and jam.
5. Brush the egg wash over the pop tarts. Place the tarts in the air fryer basket lined with parchment paper.
6. Put the air fryer lid on and bake in batches in the preheated instant pot at 375°F until golden brown, about 8 minutes.
7. Remove the tarts from the basket. Let cool for a few minutes and sprinkle with powdered sugar to serve.

HOME-STYLE APPLE ROLLS

⊕Cooking Time: 80 minutes   🎩Serves: 6

Ingredients:
- ½ stick butter, at room temperature
- 2 ¼ cups all-purpose flour
- ½ cup milk
- 1 tablespoon yeast
- ½ cup sugar, granulated
- ¼ teaspoon salt
- 1 egg, beaten
- Cooking spray

Filling:
- 1 apple, peeled, cored, and chopped
- ½ teaspoon ground cardamom
- 1 teaspoon ground cinnamon
- ¼ cup brown sugar
- ½ teaspoon ground cloves
- 3 tablespoons butter, at room temperature
- ½ cup powdered sugar

Directions:
1. Heat the milk in a microwave until warmed through. Pour the milk in the electric mixer, then mix in the yeast and granulated sugar. Whisk until the yeast bubbles. Slowly stir the milk mixture with butter in a bowl, then add the beaten egg. Put in the flour and salt. Whisk until it forms a dough. Place the dough on a lightly floured surface and knead for 5 minutes. Put the dough in a big bowl, cover and leave it in a warm place for approximately an hour.
2. Roll the dough out into a 1-inch rectangle with rolling pin. Brush the dough with 3 tablespoon of butter on both sides.
3. Mix the cardamom, cinnamon, brown sugar, and cloves in a separate bowl. Top the dough with the powder mixture and chopped apple, then roll the dough into a log. Cut the dough log into 6 equal-sized rolls.
4. Line the air fryer basket with parchment paper and spritz with cooking spray. Arrange the rolls in the air fryer basket.
5. Put the air fryer lid on and bake in the preheated instant pot at 350°F for 12 minutes. Flip the rolls over when the lid screen indicates 'TURN FOOD' halfway through. Remove the rolls from the basket. Sprinkle with powdered sugar to serve on a plate.

CRISPY CINNAMON PEAR FRITTERS

◷ Cooking Time: 20 minutes   ⬤ Serves: 4

Ingredients:
- 1 teaspoon cinnamon
- 2 pears, peeled, cored, and sliced
- ½ teaspoon ginger
- 1 tablespoon coconut oil, melted
- 2 eggs
- 1½ cups all-purpose flour
- 1 teaspoon baking powder
- A pinch of fine sea salt
- 4 tablespoons milk
- A pinch of nutmeg, grated

Directions:
1. In a mixing bowl, combine all the ingredients except slices of pear. Dredge each pear slice in the mixture to coat well.
2. Arrange the slices of pears in the air fryer basket. Put the air fryer lid on and cook in batches in the preheated instant pot at 350°F for 4 minutes. Flip them over when the lid screen indicates 'TURN FOOD'.
3. Top the pears with powdered sugar, if desired, and serve on a plate.

ALMOND CHOCOLATE MUFFINS

Cooking Time: 20 minutes   Serves: 6

Ingredients:
- ½ cup almonds, chopped
- 1½ ounces dark chocolate chunks
- 1 cup powdered sugar
- ¼ teaspoon nutmeg, preferably freshly grated
- 1 tablespoon cocoa powder
- ¼ teaspoon salt
- ¾ cup self-raising flour
- 1 egg, whisked
- ½ teaspoon vanilla extract
- 2 ounces butter, softened
- 2 tablespoons almond milk
- 6 muffin cups
- Cooking spray

Directions:
1. Combine the flour, sugar, nutmeg, cocoa powder, and salt in a bowl. Set aside.
2. Mix the whisked egg, vanilla, butter, and almond milk in another bowl. Set aside.
3. Stir the egg mixture into the flour mixture. Add the almonds and chocolate chunks. Stir to form a batter.
4. Spritz the muffin cups with cooking spray. Pour the batter into muffin cups, filling each about three-quarters full. Place the cups in the air fryer basket.
5. Put the air fryer lid on and bake in batches in the preheated instant pot at 350°F until the cake springs back when gently pressed with your fingers, about 12 minutes.
6. Remove the muffin cups from the basket. Dust with chocolate sprinkles, if desired.

WHITE CHOCOLATE LAVA CAKE

Cooking Time: 20 minutes   Serves: 4

Ingredients:
- 3 ounces white chocolate
- 2½ ounces butter, at room temperature
- 2 eggs, beaten
- ½ cup powdered sugar
- 1 teaspoon rum extract
- 1 teaspoon vanilla extract
- 1/3 cup self-rising flour
- 4 ramekins
- Cooking spray

Directions:
1. Melt the white chocolate and butter in a microwave for 15 seconds. Whisk the beaten eggs and sugar until smooth in a mixing bowl.
2. Pour the chocolate and butter mixture into the bowl of the egg mixture, then add the rum extract, vanilla extract, and flour. Stir to incorporate.
3. Spritz the ramekins with cooking spray. Pour the batter into the ramekins, filling each about three-quarters full. Transfer the ramekins into the air fryer basket.
4. Put the air fryer lid on and bake in the preheated instant pot at 375°F for 9 to 11 minutes.
5. Remove the ramekins from the air fryer basket and cool for 2 to 3 minutes. Serve warm.

ORANGE JUICY ROLLS

⊕Cooking Time: 80 minutes   Serves: 6

Ingredients:
- 2 tablespoons fresh orange juice
- 2 cups all-purpose flour
- ½ cup milk
- 1 tablespoon yeast
- ¼ cup granulated sugar
- ¼ teaspoon salt
- ½ stick butter, at room temperature
- 1 egg, at room temperature

Filling:
- 2 tablespoons butter
- 1 teaspoon ground star anise
- 1 teaspoon vanilla paste
- 4 tablespoons white sugar
- ¼ teaspoon ground cinnamon
- ½ cup confectioners' sugar

Directions:
1. Heat the milk in a microwave until warmed through, then pour the milk in the electric mixer. Mix in the yeast and granulated sugar. Whisk until the yeast is foamy. Slowly pour the milk mixture and butter into a bowl. Add the beaten egg, flour and salt. Mix well. Fold in the orange juice and blend until a smooth dough forms. Place the dough on a lightly floured surface and knead for 5 minutes. Put the dough in a big bowl. Cover with plastic wrap and leave it in a warm place for approximately an hour.
2. Roll the dough out into a 1-inch rectangle with rolling pin. Brush the dough with 2 tablespoon of butter on both sides.
3. Mix the ground star anise, vanilla, white sugar and cinnamon in a bowl. Dust the dough with the powder mixture. Roll the dough into a log and cut into 6 rolls.Line the air fryer basket with parchment paper. Arrange the rolls in the basket and spritz with cooking spray.
4. Put the air fryer lid on and bake in the preheated instant pot at 350°F for 12 minutes. Flip the rolls when the lid screen indicates 'TURN FOOD' halfway through. Remove the rolls from the basket. Sprinkle with the confectioners' sugar to serve.

OREO CHEESECAKE WITH COCONUT

Cooking Time: 25mins+chilling time/ Serves: 4

Ingredients:
- 12 ounces cream cheese
- 1 teaspoon pure coconut extract
- 1 cup toasted coconut
- 1½ cups Oreo cookies, crushed
- 4 tablespoons butter, softened
- 4 ounces sugar, granulated
- 2 eggs, lightly whisked
- 4 ounces double cream
- 1 teaspoon pure vanilla extract
- 4 silicone cupcake molds

Directions:
1. Combine the butter with crushed Oreo cookies and sugar in a bowl. Spoon the mixture into the silicone cupcake molds and press tightly.
2. Arrange the molds in the air fryer basket. Put the air fryer lid on and bake in the preheated instant pot at 350°F for 5 minutes. Transfer the molds to a cooling rack to cool.
3. Meanwhile, whisk the double cream and cream cheese in a separate bowl until well combined. Fold in the whisked eggs, coconut extract and vanilla. Stir to incorporate.
4. Top the molds with the cream cheese mixture. Return the molds to the air fryer basket and bake at 325°F for 13 to 15 minutes.
5. Remove the molds from the basket. Spread the toasted coconut on top of the molds. Leave them in the freezer to cool until ready to serve.

RUSTIC TOMATO AND BEEF OMELET WITH KALE

Cooking Time: 20 minutes   Serves: 4

Ingredients:
- 1 tomato, chopped
- ½ pound leftover beef, coarsely chopped
- 1 cup kale, torn into pieces and wilted
- 1/8 teaspoon ground allspice
- ¼ teaspoon brown sugar
- ½ teaspoon turmeric powder
- 2 garlic cloves, pressed
- 4 eggs, beaten
- 4 tablespoons heavy cream
- Salt and ground black pepper, to taste
- 4 ramekins
- Cooking spray

Directions:
1. Mix all the ingredients in a mixing bowl until well combined. Spritz the bottom of the ramekins with cooking spray. Divide the mixture among four ramekins, filling each about three-quarters full.
2. Place the ramekins in the air fryer basket. Put the air fryer lid on and bake in the preheated instant pot at 350°F for 16 minutes or until set.
3. Remove the ramekins from the basket and serve warm.

WALNUT BROWNIES

⏰Cooking Time: 35 minutes   🧢Serves: 6

Ingredients:
- Eggs – 2
- Brown sugar – 1 cup
- Vanilla – 1/2 tsp.
- Cocoa powder – 1/4 cup
- Walnuts – 1/2 cup, chopped
- All-purpose flour – 1/4 cup
- Butter – 1/2 cup, melted
- Pinch of salt

Directions:
Spray a baking dish with cooking spray and set aside. In a bowl, whisk together eggs, butter, cocoa powder, and vanilla. Add walnuts, flour, sugar, and salt and stir well. Pour batter into the baking dish. Place steam rack into the instant pot. Place baking dish on top of the steam rack. Seal pot with the air fryer lid. Select bake mode and cook at 320 F for 35 minutes. Serve.

ALMOND BUTTER BROWNIES

◷ Cooking Time: 15 minutes   ⛑ Serves: 4

Ingredients:
- Almond butter – 1/2 cup
- Vanilla – 1/2 tsp.
- Almond milk – 1 tbsp.
- Coconut sugar – 2 tbsps.
- Applesauce – 2 tbsps.
- Honey – 2 tbsps.
- Baking powder – 1/4 tsp.
- Baking soda – 1/2 tsp.
- Cocoa powder – 2 tbsps.
- Almond flour – 3 tbsps.
- Coconut oil – 1 tbsp.
- Sea salt – 1/4 tsp.

Directions:
Spray baking pan with cooking spray and set aside. In a small bowl, mix together almond flour, baking soda, baking powder, and cocoa powder and set aside. Add coconut oil and almond butter into the microwave-safe bowl and microwave until melted. Stir. Add honey, milk, coconut sugar, vanilla, and applesauce into the melted coconut oil mixture and stir well. Add flour mixture and stir to combine. Pour batter into the baking pan. Place steam rack into the instant pot. Place baking pan on top of the steam rack. Seal pot with the air fryer lid. Select bake mode and cook at 350 F for 15 minutes. Serve.

APPETIZERS AND SNACKS

CAJUN CORNFLAKE-CRUSTED CHICKEN DRUMSTICKS

⏲ Cooking Time: 30 minutes   🍳 Serves: 2

Ingredients:
- ½ cup cornflake crumbs
- 6 large chicken drumsticks
- 1 egg
- 1 tablespoon water
- ½ teaspoon garlic powder
- ½ teaspoon onion powder
- ¼ teaspoon Cajun seasoning
- ¼ teaspoon paprika
- ¼ teaspoon chili powder
- ½ teaspoon sea salt
- Salt to taste
- Cooking spray

Directions:
1. In a shallow bowl, whisk the egg with water. Set aside.
2. In a separate bowl, combine the cornflake crumbs, garlic powder, onion power, Cajun seasoning, paprika, chili powder, and ½ teaspoon sea salt. Set aside.
3. Lightly sprinkle the drumsticks with salt. Dredge each drumstick in the egg mixture, then in the cornflake mixture.
4. Spritz the air fryer basket with cooking spray. Put the chicken into the basket.
5. Put the air fryer lid on and cook in batches in the preheated instant pot at 400°F for 15 minutes. Flip the drumsticks over when the lid screen indicates 'TURN FOOD' halfway through, or until the chicken registers at least 165°F.
6. Remove the drumsticks from the basket and serve hot on a plate.

POTATO NUGGETS WITH GOCHUJANG CHEESE SAUCE

🕐 Cooking Time: 25 minutes   🧢 Serves: 4

Ingredients:
- 1 package (16-ounce) frozen bite-size potato nuggets

Guochujang Cheese Sauce:
- 1 tablespoon gochujang (Korean hot pepper paste), or more to taste
- 1 package (8-ounce) Cheddar cheese, shredded
- ½ cup heavy whipping cream
- ¼ teaspoon salt
- Cooking spray

Directions:
1. Spritz the air fryer basket with cooking spray. Place the potato nuggets in the basket.
2. Put the air fryer lid on and cook in batches in the preheated instant pot at 375°F for 15 minutes or until golden brown on both sides. Shake the basket when the lid screen indicates 'TURN FOOD' halfway through.
3. Meanwhile, to make gochujang cheese sauce, heat the Cheddar cheese and cream in a saucepan over medium high heat. Keep stirring for about 5 minutes or until the cheese is melted. Add the gochujang and salt. Stir to combine well.
4. Remove the potato nuggets from the basket and drizzle with the sauce before serving.

VEGAN POTATO TAQUITOS

⏱ Cooking Time: 50 minutes   🎩 Serves: 6

Ingredients:
- 1 large russet potato, peeled
- 2 tablespoons onions, diced
- 6 corn tortillas
- 1 garlic clove, minced
- ¼ cup plant-based butter, melted
- 2 tablespoons unsweetened, plain almond milk
- Salt and ground black pepper to taste
- 6 corn tortillas
- Pestle and mortar
- Cooking spray

Directions:
1. Put the russet potato in a pot of salted water. Bring to a boil, then simmer over medium-low heat for 20 minutes or until tender.
2. Meanwhile, and the onions into a skillet and sauté for 3 to 5 minutes or until soft, then add the garlic and cook for 1 minute or until fragrant. Set aside.
3. Remove the potato from the pot to the pestle and mortar. Stir in the butter and almond milk. Season lightly with salt and pepper, then mash the mixture. Add the cooked onion and garlic until well combined. Set aside.
4. In a skillet, heat the tortillas until soft. Transfer to a lightly floured surface. Scoop 3 tablespoons of potato mixture onto the center of each tortilla. Fold and roll up tightly.
5. Arrange the tortillas in the air fryer basket. Mist with cooking spray.
6. Put the air fryer lid on and cook in batches in the preheated instant pot at 400°F for 6 to 9 minutes or until golden brown. Flip the tortillas when the air fry lid screen indicates 'TURN FOOD' and cook for another 3 to 5 minutes.
7. Remove the cooked tortillas (taquitos) from the basket and serve on a plate.

GOLDEN FRIES WITH WHITE CHEDDAR CHEESE SAUCE

Cooking Time: 30 minutes   Serves: 2

Ingredients:
- 2 large russet potatoes, peeled and cut into ½-inch sticks
- 2 tablespoons vegetable oil
- 1 tablespoon Old Bay Seasoning

White Cheddar Cheese Sauce:
- 2 tablespoons butter
- 2 tablespoons flour
- 1 cup milk
- ½ cup white Cheddar cheese, grated
- ½ teaspoon nutmeg
- ½ teaspoon salt
- Freshly ground black pepper, to taste

Directions:
1. Add a touch of salt to a pot of water and bring to a boil. Put the potato sticks into the pot, and blanch for 4 minutes. Remove them from the pot, allow to cool, then pat dry.
2. On a clean work surface, brush the potato sticks with the vegetable oil, then arrange them into the air fryer basket.
3. Put the air fryer lid on and cook in the preheated instant pot at 400°F for 16 minutes or until golden brown. Shake the basket three or four times during cooking time.
4. Meanwhile, put the butter into a saucepan and heat over medium-high heat for 1 minute or until the butter melts.
5. Add the flour to the saucepan. Stir and cook for 1 minute. Mix in the milk. Keep stirring to make sure it cooks evenly. Simmer the mixture until thickened.
6. Turn off the heat, and whisk in the Cheddar cheese, nutmeg, salt, and black pepper. Stir well to combine. Transfer to a serving bowl until ready to use.
7. Sprinkle the potato sticks with the Old Bay Seasoning. Put the lid on and cook for another 3 minutes.
8. Remove the fries from the basket and serve with the white Cheddar cheese sauce.

CHEESY SPINACH PHYLLO TRIANGLES

⏱ Cooking Time: 40 minutes   🔔 Serves: 8 to 10

Ingredients:

- ¼ cup Parmesan cheese, grated
- ¾ cup feta cheese, crumbled
- ½ package (10-ounce) frozen spinach, thawed and squeezed dry (about 1 cup)
- 6 sheets phyllo dough, wrapped in plastic with a damp kitchen towel on top
- ⅛ teaspoon ground nutmeg
- ¼ cup pine nuts, toasted
- 1 egg, lightly beaten
- ½ teaspoon salt
- Freshly ground black pepper, to taste
- ½ cup butter, melted

Directions:

1. In a large bowl, mix the spinach, cheeses, nutmeg, pine nuts, beaten egg, salt, and pepper.
2. Remove a sheet of phyllo dough from the plastic to a clean surface and brush over with melted butter. Then top with another sheet of phyllo dough and brush over with melted butter. Cut it into six 3-inch-wide strips.
3. Arrange a tablespoon of spinach mixture onto the middle of each strip. Fold a corner over the mixture and form the strip into a triangle, then fold the triangle once more to make it into a half-sized triangle. Repeat with the remaining phyllo dough and spinach mixture.
4. Brush the triangles with butter on all sides and arrange them into the air fryer basket.
5. Put the air fryer lid on and cook in batches in the preheated instant pot at 350°F for 10 minutes. Flip them when the lid screen indicates 'TURN FOOD' halfway through the cooking time.
6. Remove from the basket and serve warm.

POTATO CHIPS WITH SOUR CREAM DIP

⊕ Cooking Time: 30 minutes　　🧢 Serves:　2

Ingredients:
- 2 russet potatoes, rinsed, drained, and sliced, about ⅛-inch thick
- Sea salt and freshly ground black pepper, to taste
- Cooking spray

Sour Cream Dip:
- ½ cup sour cream
- ¼ teaspoon salt
- ¼ teaspoon lemon juice
- 1 tablespoon olive oil
- 2 scallions, white part only minced
- Freshly ground black pepper, to taste

Directions:
1. To make the potato chips, put the potato slices into a bowl of cold water and soak for 10 minutes. Remove from the water and pat dry with paper towels.
2. Spritz the air fryer basket with cooking spray. Arrange the potato slices in the basket (without overlapping) and spritz them with cooking spray. You may need to work in batches to avoid overcrowding.
3. Put the air fryer lid on and cook in the preheated instant at 300°F for 13 minutes or until golden brown. Flip the potato slices several times during cooking time. Sprinkle with salt and pepper and cook for another 2 minutes.
4. Meanwhile, combine all the ingredients for the sour cream dip in a serving bowl.
5. Remove the potato chips from the basket. Allow to cool for a few minutes and serve with the dip.

MELTED CHEESE SANDWICH

Cooking Time: 15 minutes   Serves: 1

Ingredients:
- 2 slices raisin bread
- 2 teaspoons honey mustard
- 3 (3-ounce) slices ham
- 4 (3-ounce) slices Muenster cheese
- 2 tablespoons butter, softened
- 2 toothpicks, soak in water for 30 minutes

Directions:
1. Lay the bread slices on a clean work surface, cover one side of each slice of bread with honey mustard. Assemble the bread slices with ham slices and cheese slices in between the honey mustard sides to make a sandwich.
2. Spread the butter on the outside of the sandwich, secure with 2 toothpicks, and then place it in the air fryer basket
3. Put the air fryer lid on and cook in the preheated instant pot at 375°F for 10 minutes. Flip the sandwich when the lid screen indicates 'TURN FOOD' halfway through the cooking time.
4. Remove the sandwich from the basket. Let it cool, and discard the toothpick before serving.

VEGGIES AND SHRIMP ROLLS

⊕Cooking Time: 20 minutes　　🎩Serves:　8

Ingredients:
- 8 egg roll wrappers
- Cooking spray

Filling:
- 1 pound cooked shrimp, diced
- 1 cup carrots, shredded
- 1 cup fresh bean sprouts, drained
- ½ head green or savoy cabbage, finely shredded
- ¼ cup hoisin sauce, and more to serve (optional)
- 1 tablespoon soy sauce
- ½ teaspoon sugar
- Freshly ground black pepper, to taste
- 1 teaspoon sesame oil
- ¼ cup scallions
- 1 tablespoon vegetable oil

Directions:
1. To make the filling, warm the vegetable oil in a frying pan over medium-high heat, then add the carrots, bean sprouts, and cabbage. Sauté for 3 minutes until wilted. Mix in the hoisin sauce, soy sauce, sugar, black pepper, and sesame oil. Sauté for 3 minutes more, then add the scallions and shrimp. Sauté until fork-tender. Allow to cool. Put the filling into a colander. Drain the water out of the filling. Set the dried filling aside.
2. To make the shrimp rolls, arrange each egg wrapper on a lightly floured cutting board, pointing a corner towards you.
3. Evenly divide and spoon the filling on the center of each wrapper, leaving a 2-inch space between the filling and the border of the each wrapper.
4. Brush the 2-inch space of one wrapper with a touch of water. Fold the corner towards you over the filling, fold the right and left corners toward the center. Tuck the corner over the filling to form a roll. Press to seal. Repeat with the remaining wrappers and filling.
5. Spritz the air fryer basket with cooking spray. Arrange the rolls in the air fryer basket, and spritz them with cooking spray. You may need to work in batches to avoid overcrowding. Put the air fryer lid on and cook in the preheated instant pot at 375°F for 10 minutes. Flip the rolls when the lid screen indicates 'TURN FOOD' halfway through.
6. Remove from the basket and serve with hoisin sauce, if desired.

THE BLOSSOM OF ONION

⊕Cooking Time: 25 minutes   ▲Serves: 2

Ingredients:
- 1 large sweet onion, peeled, leaving the root intact
- 2 eggs
- ½ cup milk
- 1 cup flour
- ½ teaspoon garlic powder
- ¼ teaspoon ground cayenne pepper
- ½ teaspoon paprika
- 1 teaspoon salt
- ½ teaspoon freshly ground black pepper
- Cooking spray

Dipping Sauce:
- ½ tablespoon ketchup
- ½ tablespoon mayonnaise
- ½ teaspoon paprika
- ½ teaspoon onion powder
- ½ teaspoon ground cayenne pepper
- 1 teaspoon Worcestershire sauce

Directions:
1. Cut about 1-inch off top of the onion. Put the onion on a cutting board, root side up.Use the knife tip to slice 16 slits around the onion, starting half an inch from the root. You can slice the onion around by following the direction at 3, 6, 9, and 12 o'clock , then in the four spaces between each of these slits, slice another three more slits.
2. Turn the onion over and let the flower bloom. Then discard the loose petals in the center of the onion. Arrange in a large bowl, sliced side up.
3. In a second bowl, whisk together the eggs and milk. Mix the flour, garlic powder, cayenne pepper, paprika, salt, and black pepper in a third bowl.
4. Dust the onion flower with half of the dry mixture, then gentle shake the excess off. Place the onion into the egg mixture and soak for 1 minute. Gently shake the excess off. Transfer the onion back to the first bowl and dust with the dry mixture again. Gently shake the excess off.
5. Spritz the air fryer basket with cooking spray. Arrange the well-coated onion flower into the air fryer basket, and spritz it with cooking spray.
6. Put the air fryer lid on and air fry in the preheated instant pot at 350°F for 25

minutes. Spritz with cooking spray at least two more times during cooking time. Meanwhile, mix all the ingredients for the dipping sauce together. Remove the onion flower from the basket and serve with the dipping sauce.

MOST POPULAR AIR FRYER LID RECIPES

VEGGIES AND BEEF OMELET

Cooking Time: 20 minutes   Serves: 4

Ingredients:
- ½ pound leftover beef, coarsely chopped
- 1 tomato, chopped
- 1 cup kale, torn into pieces and wilted
- ⅛ teaspoon ground allspice
- ¼ teaspoon brown sugar
- ½ teaspoon turmeric powder
- 2 garlic cloves, pressed
- 4 eggs, beaten
- 4 tablespoons heavy cream
- Salt and ground black pepper, to taste
- 4 ramekins
- Cooking spray

Directions:
1. To make the omelet, mix all the ingredients in a mixing bowl until well combined. Spritz the bottom and sides of the ramekins with cooking spray. Divide the mixture among four ramekins.
2. Place the ramekins in the air fryer basket. Put the air fryer lid on and bake in the preheated instant pot at 350°F for 16 minutes.
3. Remove the ramekins from the basket and serve warm.

SPICY BEEF SPAGHETTI

⊕Cooking Time: 35 minutes   Serves: 4

Ingredients:
- 1 pound spaghetti
- 1 onion, peeled and finely chopped
- ¾ pound ground beef chuck
- ½ teaspoon dried marjoram
- ½ teaspoon dried rosemary
- 1 teaspoon garlic paste
- 1 small-sized habanero pepper, deveined and finely minced
- 1 bell pepper, chopped
- 1¼ cups tomatoes, crushed
- ¼ teaspoon ground black pepper, or more to taste
- ½ teaspoon sea salt flakes
- Cooking spray

Directions:
1. Bring a pot of water to a boil. Put in the spaghetti and cook over medium-high heat until al dente. Transfer the spaghetti in a serving platter. Set aside.
2. Spritz a 6×6×2 inch pan with cooking spray. Put the onion, ground meat, marjoram, rosemary, garlic paste, habanero pepper, and bell pepper in the pan. Stir to mix well.
3. Arrange the pan in the air fryer basket. Put the air fryer lid on and cook in the preheated instant pot at 375°F for 20 minutes. Whisk in the tomatoes, pepper, and salt halfway through. Stir periodically.
4. Remove the pan from the basket. Spoon the mixture on top of the cooked spaghetti. Stir to serve.

HOMEMADE LONDON BROIL

Cooking Time: 35 minutes   Serves: 8

Ingredients:
- 2 pounds London broil, rinsed and drained
- ½ teaspoon dried hot red pepper flakes
- 2 tablespoons olive oil
- 3 large garlic cloves, minced
- 3 tablespoons balsamic vinegar
- 3 tablespoons whole-grain mustard
- Sea salt and ground black pepper, to taste

Directions:
1. Cut several silts on both sides of the London broil.
2. Mix the remaining ingredients well in a bowl. Dunk the London broil into the mixture. Wrap in plastic and refrigerate to marinate for at least 3 hours.
3. Discard the marinade. Shake the excess off. Arrange the London broil in the air fryer basket.
4. Put the air fryer lid on and cook in the preheated instant pot at 375°F for 20 minutes, flipping the London broil once when it shows 'TURN FOOD' on the air fryer lid screen halfway through.
5. Transfer the cooked London broil to a platter and serve.

CLASSIC BEEF STROGANOFF

Cooking Time: 20 minutes   Serves: 4

Ingredients:
- ¾ pound beef sirloin steak, cut into small-sized strips
- 1 tablespoon brown mustard
- ¼ cup balsamic vinegar
- 2 tablespoons all-purpose flour
- 1 tablespoon olive oil
- 1 cup leeks, chopped
- 2 cloves garlic, crushed
- 1 cup beef broth
- Sea salt and red pepper flakes, crushed, to taste
- 2½ tablespoons tomato paste
- 1 teaspoon cayenne pepper
- 1 cup sour cream

Directions:
1. In a bowl, combine the beef strips with the mustard and balsamic vinegar. Wrap in plastic and refrigerate to marinate for at least 1 hour.
2. Meanwhile, prepare a separate bowl of flour.
3. Discard the marinade. Dredge the beef strips in the flour to coat well.
4. Grease a 6-inch baking dish with the olive oil. Arrange the beef strips in the basket. Add the leeks, garlic and broth. Stir to combine, and arrange the dish into the air fryer basket.
5. Put the air fryer lid on and bake in the preheated instant pot at 375°F for 16 minutes. Sprinkle with the red pepper flakes, salt, tomato paste, cayenne pepper, and sour cream halfway through the cooking time or until lightly browned.
6. Remove the beef strips from the basket and serve in a large bowl.

RUSTIC PORK MEATLOAF

Cooking Time: 30 minutes   Serves: 4

Ingredients:

- ½ pound lean pork, minced
- ⅓ teaspoon dried basil
- ½ tablespoon fish sauce
- ½ teaspoon dried thyme
- ½ tablespoon green garlic, minced
- 1½ tablespoons fresh cilantro, minced
- 2 leeks, chopped
- 2 tablespoons tomato puree
- Salt and ground black pepper, to taste
- ⅓ cup bread crumbs
- 1 tablespoon olive oil

Directions:

1. Place all the ingredients, except the bread crumbs, into a large bowl. Stir to mix well. Shape the mixture into a meatloaf.
2. Combine the bread crumbs with olive oil in a separate bowl. Dunk the meatloaf into the bowl to coat well. Arrange the meatloaf in the air fryer basket.
3. Put the air fryer lid on and cook in the preheated instant pot at 375°F for 20 minutes or until cooked through. Flip the meatloaf when the lid screen indicates 'TURN FOOD' halfway through the cooking time.
4. Remove the meatloaf from the basket. Let stand for 10 minutes and slice to serve.

CRISPY PORK CHOPS

◷ Cooking Time: 30 minutes   ◖ Serves: 6

Ingredients:

- 6 pork chops
- ⅓ teaspoon freshly cracked black pepper
- 1 teaspoon seasoned salt
- Garlic and onion spice blend, to taste
- 2 teaspoons Cajun seasoning
- 3 tablespoons white flour
- 2 eggs
- ⅓ cup Italian bread crumbs
- 1 tablespoon olive oil
- Fresh cilantro, roughly chopped, to taste

Directions:

1. Mix the pepper, salt, spice blend, and Cajun seasoning together in a bowl. Dunk the pork chops in the mixture. Wrap in plastic and refrigerate to marinate for at least 3 hours.
2. Place the flour into a second bowl. Beat the egg in a third bowl until smooth and frothy. Combine the Italian bread crumbs and olive oil in a fourth bowl.
3. Dip the pork chops in the flour, then in the egg, and then in the bread crumbs. Arrange the well coated pork chops in the basket.
4. Put the air fryer lid on and cook the pork chops in batches in the preheated instant pot at 350°F for 18 minutes. Flip the pork chops when the lid screen indicates 'TURN FOOD' halfway through.
5. Transfer the cooked pork chops to a platter. Sprinkle with fresh cilantro for garnish, then serve.

BACON-WRAPPED ONION RING

Cooking Time: 25 minutes   Serves: 6

Ingredients:
- 12 rashers of back bacon
- 2 onions, sliced into rings
- ½ teaspoon ground black pepper
- ½ teaspoon salt
- ½ teaspoon chili powder
- ½ teaspoon paprika
- ½ tablespoon soy sauce
- Fresh parsley, chopped, to taste

Directions:
1. In a bowl, combine the black pepper, salt, chili powder, and paprika. Dunk the onion rings in the mixture. Refrigerate to marinate for 20 minutes.
2. Wrap 2 slices of bacon through the middle of each onion ring and fully twine to cover, leaving the center of the ring open. Sprinkle with the soy sauce.
3. Arrange the rings in the air basket. Put the air fryer lid on and cook in batches in the preheated instant pot at 350°F for 16 minutes. Flip the rings when the lid screen indicates 'TURN FOOD' halfway through.
4. Remove the rings from the basket. Sprinkle with fresh parsley to serve.

GREEK ROASTED FIGS

◷Cooking Time: 20 minutes   ▬Serves: 4

Ingredients:
- 8 figs, halved
- 2 teaspoons butter, melted
- ½ teaspoon cinnamon
- 1 teaspoon lemon zest
- 2 tablespoons brown sugar
- 4 tablespoons honey
- 1 cup Greek yogurt
- Cooking spray

Directions:
1. In a bowl, combine the melted butter, cinnamon, lemon zest, and brown sugar. Dredge the fig halves in the mixture to coat well.
2. Spritz the air fryer basket with cooking spray. Arrange the fig halves in the basket. Put the air fryer lid on and roast in the preheated instant pot at 325°F for 16 minutes. Flip the figs when the lid screen indicates 'TURN FOOD' halfway through.
3. In the meantime, combine the honey with the Greek yogurt in a separate bowl.
4. Transfer the figs into 4 bowls evenly and serve with the yogurt sauce.

AIR-FRIED EGG AND SAUSAGE MUFFIN

Cooking Time: 25 minutes   Serves: 6

Ingredients:
- 6 eggs, beaten
- ½ pound turkey sausage
- 1 teaspoon lard or butter
- 1 chili pepper, deseeded and chopped
- 1 sweet pepper, deseeded and chopped
- 1 garlic clove, minced
- 1 scallion, chopped
- ½ cup Swiss cheese, shredded
- Sea salt and ground black pepper, to taste
- Cooking spray

Directions:
1. In a saucepan, add the lard and melt over medium-high heat. Add and saute the sausage for 5 minutes or until lightly browned.
2. Remove the sausage from the basket to a cutting board. Cut the sausage into small pieces.
3. Combine the sausage, beaten eggs, chili pepper, sweet pepper, garlic,scallion, salt, and pepper in a bowl.
4. Use cooking spray to spritz a 6-cup muffin tin. Spoon the sausage mixture into the muffin tin. Sprinkle with the shredded cheese.
5. Arrange the muffin tin in the air fryer basket. Put the air fryer lid on and co in the preheated instant pot at 350°F for 12 minutes, flipping the mixture once with a skewer when the lid screen indicates 'TURN FOOD' halfway through the cooking time.
6. Remove the muffin tin from the basket and serve warm.

ok

9 781649 840899